Ajit Singh Dutta (1944-2022) was born and raised in Jamshedpur, India. After finishing his university studies in India, he moved to England to pursue his professional credentials, becoming a Fellow of the Institute of Chartered Accountants. He lived and worked on four continents, ultimately settling in the US where he received an MBA from the George Washington University, and owned a successful financial management consulting company. Ajit also received an MFA degree in 2016 from the University of California, Riverside. Throughout his life, he pursued his passion of writing, poetry and photography. Ajit is a published poet in English, with *A Father's Poems* (2000) and other works of his having been anthologized. His book of translated Urdu ghazals, *A Lover's Sigh*, was published in 2021. Ajit passed away in 2022 and is survived by his wife, Bonnie Galat, and his daughters, Danielle and Nikki Dutta.

MY FATHER'S RING

The Story of a Lost Romance

Ajit Singh Dutta

SPEAKING TIGER

SPEAKING TIGER BOOKS LLP
125A, Ground Floor, Shahpur Jat, near Asiad Village,
New Delhi 110049

First published in India by Speaking Tiger Books 2023

ISBN: 978-93-5447-576-4
eISBN: 978-93-5447-594-8

10 9 8 7 6 5 4 3 2 1

Typeset in Nebraska by SÜRYA, New Delhi
Printed at HT Media Ltd, Greater Noida

CONTENTS

PART THREE

AUTHOR'S NOTE

The story I am about to tell you, about the passionate love between an American pianist/composer and a Sikh engineer in the 1920s, is true.

Truth, however, is predicated on perspective and memory, for affairs of the heart are not empirical, and both these sources are unreliable at their core. One is subject to parallax; the other is filtered through our own biases. In other words, both could be untrustworthy.

Nevertheless, these are what I had in hand as I began to write. In addition, I had letters from the two protagonists. She wrote extensively and passionately to him. He wrote to his brother.

Where the letters provide facts about what happened and where, I have used them as the basis for dialogue and scenes. I was fortunate, too, in having descendants of the lovers to help me fill in their personalities, to shade them in more truthful ways.

In addition, I did a lot of research on the time and places in which these events unfolded.

The sum of these—the protagonists' own words, their descendants' memories, and my own research—form the basis of the story. If it succeeds in being believable, I have done my job. If it does not, I acknowledge my shortcomings.

PROLOGUE

27 March 1928, Brooklyn's Pier 1

The clerk at the ticket booth of the Ellerman & Bucknall Steamship line had not seen many Sikhs in his life. But there, right in front of him, was Raj, with his light grey-blue turban and black beard. The clerk stared, and Raj stared back, unperturbed. Next to Raj, holding his arm, was a beautiful American woman, expensively dressed; she was also staring at the clerk as though daring him to say something. She looked at him haughtily, but the clerk could see that her eyes were red, her cheeks tear-stained.

Raj pulled out his passport and handed it to the clerk. He also presented the ticket he'd purchased from an agent in Chicago for his passage to Karachi, India. Behind and around him, Raj could hear the bustle of the pier.

The clerk addressed him: 'Well, Sir, you know you're on the *S.S. City of Lahore*, right?'

'Yes, I know.'

'And your passage is to Karachi, via Marseilles. Second class.'

'Yes, Karachi.'

'Good luck to you, then.' With that, the clerk stamped the ticket and returned it, along with Raj's passport. But then he paused.

'Wait. I think I have something for you,' he said, hunting in the cubby holes around him. With a triumphant flourish, he plucked out an envelope and handed it to Raj.

'This came for you, Sir, only this morning. That's why I remembered it. Lucky for you.'

Raj looked at the cream-coloured envelope and recognized it as one of a set that Louise had bought.

The envelope was typed with his details:

Mr Rajinder Singh Datta
Care of S.S. 'City of Lahore'
Sailing March 27th
Pier No. One
Foot of 51st Street
Brooklyn
N.Y.

He turned to the woman on his arm and said, 'From you, Louise?'

A pang of remorse hit him as Louise clutched his arm more tightly.

'If I hadn't been able to come here with you, I wanted you to know I was still with you,' she said.

Raj put his arms around her shoulders and nodded silently. 'You're always with me and always will be.'

The clerk, who had not seen many interracial couples, leaned forward, and pointed out a low-slung ship with a black funnel in the centre of its deck. The top of the funnel was circled by six white diamonds, three of which were visible from any angle.

'That's your ship, Sir, the *S.S. City of Lahore.* It will leave shortly. You best get on board. The man in the white cap and armband at the top of the ramp will show you to the second-class lounge.'

Raj looked glumly at his home for the next few weeks. He was not looking forward to the uncomfortable quarters—especially since he'd just completed an arduous trip. Raj and Louise had travelled some twenty hours from Chicago's La Salle station to New York's Grand Central on the 20th Century Limited—which advertised itself as 'The Most Famous Train in the World'. Famous perhaps, Raj thought, but not very pleasant.

Louise had insisted on coming with him to Brooklyn, over his protestations. 'You promised you'll be back in two years,' she'd said. 'Let me at least get a few more hours with you.'

Now she turned to him and asked if he had his passport and ticket. 'And make sure your money is in a safe place,' she warned.

Raj held her and said, 'I'm OK. Don't worry about me. But what about you? Will you be all right?'

She laughed, but a little wildly. 'Oh, sure, I'll be fine. You worry about getting back to India and your family.'

Then she clutched him more fiercely, inviting curious looks from the other passengers: here was an attractive, imposing, American woman, fashionably attired, with a turbaned man wearing a threadbare blue suit, a battered suitcase at his feet.

Raj and Louise didn't seem to notice. She dug around in her handbag and handed him a small bundle.

'You remember when you traced the route of your journey back to India, and we calculated the time it would take to get from New York to Quetta? We said forty days, right?'

He nodded. The steamship would take him from New York to Marseilles, then on to India via Alexandria, through the Suez Canal, and to Karachi. From there, the Mail train would carry him to Quetta, covering some 600 miles in three or four days.

'How I wish I could go with you,' Louise was saying. 'But if I can't…well, open the bundle.'

He did and saw a large number of sealed envelopes, held together by a rubber band, all in that same cream colour as the one the ticketing agent had just given him.

'What's this?' he asked.

'I didn't want you to be alone. So, I wrote a letter for each day of your journey. There are forty in all. But promise you'll only read one letter a day. That way a part of me will be with you the whole time.'

'You did this for me? But how did you find so much to write?'

'There's no news in it, darling, just echoes of my love and of my heart's beat, as I wait for you to come back. It was easy to write. I think of you, and only you, day, and night. My feelings are for you. Promise you'll read only one letter each day.'

Struggling to control his emotions, Raj managed to say, 'Yes I will,' in a hoarse whisper.

'And now, darling, open this,' she said, handing him a velvet pouch with a gold tasselled drawstring around it. Reaching inside, he found a small velvet box. Inside the box was a ring.

'This is so beautiful. Is it a ruby?'

'Yes, it is—a cabochon ruby. You see, there are no facets on it. Just the one. Just as there is only one person and one face for me—yours! Try it on. You never wear jewellery, but I think you'll like this.'

He did as she asked. The ring fit on his third finger.

'How did you know my ring size?'

'Ah, that was devious. Remember how I tied a knot on your finger once saying it was to remind you of my concert date? Well, when you slipped it off, I saved it. I took it to the jewellers in downtown Chicago and asked them for a ruby ring. Rubies, as you know, come mainly from Burma, and I thought that was close enough to India to be the gem for my Eastern man. Do you like it?'

'It's beautiful. I'll keep it forever.'

'Yes, keep it forever and don't forget me.' She paused. 'And I'll keep the box with the attar of roses you gave me last night. 'I'll take it out every day, and smell one of the six vials. The scent will keep you close to me.' She looked as though she might tear up again. He looked into her eyes and shook his head. 'I'll come back. Don't cry.'

The porter was shouting 'All Aboard.' She kissed him tenderly and said, 'Now, go. I love you.'

Shoving the bundle of letters into his suit pocket, Raj wiped his eyes with the cuff of his suit. He picked up his suitcase and pushed his way up the ramp to the ship's deck. After he had stowed his case, he went back outside. He looked for her on the dock, and saw she was waving a handkerchief. He waved back. She blew him a kiss.

The ship's horn had blasted a warning. Slowly, the ship slipped out of the dock and turned ever so gently towards the east. Almost five years ago, he thought, five years since I landed in San Francisco and began my American journey. Now I'm leaving, with a degree and a job lined up back home. But I've lost my heart.

As he leaned forward on the railing, he saw her tiny figure on the pier waving frantically. She got smaller and smaller. He walked back to the ship's stern to keep her in sight. As he leaned forward on the rail, he patted his pocket and felt the bundle of her letters. He would write to her from Marseilles and then from Port Said.

The ship had turned left. Behind him the pier disappeared and, along with it, Louise's figure. He could see the Statue of Liberty in the distance, lighting his way.

Once the voyage was underway, the days became monotonous, and the weather acquired a steely grey mantle. He was becoming morose. How will I fit in in India after five years in America, he wondered.

As promised, each day he took out one of her letters and read and re-read it. The letters comforted him. On the fourth day out of New York, and halfway to Marseilles, he took out Letter No. 4. He read it slowly.

My Darling Jindra,

What shall I give you today, of all that my heart holds in store for you? Shall I conceal the ache that permeates every thought of you (that is to say, the ache which fills my mind, since I think of nothing but you!)—and try to banter gaily, to conceal what is so ever-present? I think not—for you would not be deceived, would you, man of my heart? Knowing my overwhelming love for you, you cannot but understand my sadness—you must want me to mourn, even as I, loving you, rejoice that I am able to feel your loss so keenly. Since you must go, I glory in the agony I feel at your departure. If the time should come (as I suppose it must, this being the way of humanity) where I shall miss you less poignantly—I shall hate the surcease of pain Jindraji. I want to pine and die of my need of you. There's only one thing I want more: this: I want not to try to hold you against your will. I write this, knowing that I shall see you many more times—several more, at any rate! May God keep me from attempting to force you to stay here! From every point-of-view, that would be disastrous. If I should succeed, I would lose respect for you: if I were to fail, I should have no more confidence in my powers of persuasion—and the whole scheme would be fundamentally wrong. No—I think I shall have strength enough not to succumb to that temptation and if, reading this, you are able to think back, 'She did try'—Oh forgive it, darling. If ever I do that thing, it will be when I have lost my mind, with grief over this ghastly separation, this terrible pulling apart of Jindralooesy.

For here is a poem which expresses what I feel:

SONG FOR ADONIS

Not every woman is a selfish child,
Who longs to bind you with some stupid tie;
To some, you are a glorious sunset sky,
The sea's low music or a song bird's trill,
A rare flower growing on some barren hill,
To thrill at, fill one's heart with, then pass by.

ROMANDRA.

Goodbye—for today—my dear—my dear.
Looesy

Turning his face into the wind, with his back to the passengers on deck, he wept freely.

He looked down at his finger, at the ring she had given him.

In the light, it gleamed back at him. Its ruby-pink colour was mysterious, alluring, and bright, all at the same time. She was with him, and he would treasure it always.

I have that ring. My father gave it to me.

The ruby is half an inch wide, positioned sideways across my finger, embraced and bezel-set in gold. The ruby is finished, I learned later, as a cabochon gem: that is, it has been shaped and polished but has not been faceted. It has a domed top and a flat bottom. It is rather handsome.

To the appraiser in Washington, DC, to whom I had taken the ring in the 1980s, the ring was just a 'gent's yellow gold ring set with an elongated cabochon ruby'. Yet that cryptic description doesn't do it justice; neither does it account for the many people who have come up to me over the years to compliment the ring's beauty. It wasn't the appraiser's job to wax poetic over its pomegranate colour, its intense glow, the simplicity of its design but aesthetic cohesiveness, the jewellery maker's obvious pleasure in his art. While the appraiser got the carats right, the mystery of the ring escaped him.

Just as, for many years, it escaped me.

Part One

ONE

Jamshedpur, Early 1950s

I remember the day my father gave the ring to me. All seven of us, my parents, myself and my four siblings, were seated on the large veranda of our house in Jamshedpur, the industrial city, famous for its steel plant which was the largest in India. Before us lay a battered, grey painted tin box with a padlock. The box had a series of numbers written on its lid in black paint. The keyhole to the padlock was covered in a red seal with a stamp on it. It also had a wire looped through the hasp with yet another number printed on it.

It was a safety deposit box, my father explained to us, that had made a long journey from Quetta, in Pakistan, to us in Jamshedpur: a journey of over a thousand miles from a bank there to the State Bank of India's branch in Bistupur, the main market of Jamshedpur.

Many years earlier, in 1934, my father had left his hometown of Quetta, a rough-and-tumble frontier town in Baluchistan, near the border between pre-partitioned India and Afghanistan. An engineer, he had recently completed his contract with Bucyrus Erie, an American heavy equipment manufacturing company, engaged in constructing the Sukkur Barrage in Sind across the Indus River, and now the border between India and Pakistan. Leaving Quetta, he had gone south-eastwards, to Jamshedpur, to start a new life. He had a new job in the steel mills there as their first Indian manager. The company had provided him the comfortable bungalow we lived in.

In 1937, he had returned to Quetta to marry my mother in an arranged marriage that took place in my mother's hometown of Bhaun, also now in Pakistan.

Together they went to Jamshedpur, leaving behind most of my mother's trousseau and almost all my father's valuables. These items were put in a safety deposit box and deposited in a bank in Quetta. The journey was long and arduous, and they felt it was safer to leave the valuables in Quetta and retrieve them later in bits and pieces.

While they did go back to Quetta from time to time, they were never able to bring back all their valuables. When they had left Quetta, it was part of undivided India.

In many ways, it was just as well that my parents left before the Partition. The unceremonious and abrupt division of India and the creation of Pakistan tore apart the subcontinent in a bloody outpouring of hate. Over 10 million people crossed the new border: Sikhs and Hindus left the new Pakistan for temporary housing with friends and relatives, or for refugee camps, in India, while Muslims left India to go to Pakistan. Miles of angry and wretched people, with their hastily bundled belongings clutched tightly, filed past each other in opposite directions. As often as not, the rage they felt over lost homes and possessions boiled over into bloodshed. There were reports of trains pulling into stations on both sides of the border entirely filled with dead bodies. Homes were ransacked. Rapes, murders, pillaging, looting: all were commonplace. This communal hatred left more than a million people dead in its wake. The violent nature of Partition created an atmosphere of mutual hostility and suspicion between India and Pakistan that has played out in three wars since.

It was in these uncertain times that my parents' holdings, along with all other holdings in banks on both sides of the Ravi River, were frozen. It was only in the early 1950s, after relations between India and Pakistan had normalized somewhat, that the countries agreed to exchange these frozen assets.

~

Mr Nanda, the manager of the State Bank of India, and a close friend of our family, had called earlier that day to inform my father of the box's arrival. My father invited him to tea that evening, and Mr Nanda brought the box home to us, driving up in his chauffeured, though tiny, British-made Morris Minor.

His chauffeur brought in the box and placed it in on a table in front of my mother. He also brought with him a large, nasty looking bolt cutter for the padlock and a saw in case the cutter did not work. With a nod from Mr Nanda, who made sure that he showed my parents that the seal and the padlock were intact, the driver clasped the box's padlock firmly in the jaws of the cutter and cut through the hasp. It was only after the driver was sent back to the car that Mr Nanda asked my father to open the box. Both my parents were instructed to inspect the contents. Satisfied with whatever they saw, they closed the lid and nodded to Mr Nanda who handed my father a piece of paper to sign.

'You're lucky,' Mr Nanda said, 'that the governments decided to exchange these frozen locker boxes. Otherwise, like all other assets left behind, they too would have been looted. You can thank the State Bank for prevailing on both countries to release the boxes.' With that, Mr Nanda said his goodbyes and left with an enthusiastic wave.

Our family gathered around this box, anxiously waiting to see what it contained.

It was a familiar yet noteworthy scene at our home in Jamshedpur that early evening. The detritus of teatime was all around us on the veranda: platters of fiery, deep-fried pakoras made with potatoes, cauliflowers and even nasturtium flowers freshly plucked from our garden, bottles of homemade chutneys and pickles, spicy keema samosas, sweet and savoury poodas, biscuits, different varieties of milk-based sweetmeats only Indians seem destined to relish, and, of course, two large teapots brewing Darjeeling, nestled under their cosies. Tea was a ritual and a full meal, and we all relished it.

The seven of us usually took all our meals together,

and tea was an important event. All of us would have reassembled at home from our various activities—my father from work, my mother from her All India Women's Conference or similar meetings or an afternoon of conversing with neighbours, and my siblings and I from school and school-run compulsory sports. Teatime was for exchanging the day's happenings. Ahead lay the evening.

Now, before us was the open safety box with its contents on display: necklaces, bracelets, jewellery sets, rings, earrings, silver rupees, crumpled notes, documents, gold sovereigns, Ashrafi and Mohur coins. Most of the jewellery was in its own original box lined with a velvety looking cloth. The names of the jewellers were embossed in gold on the lid of each box. As each piece was taken out of its box, there was a joyous cry from my mother as she recognized the reddish-yellow gleam of 22-karat gold ornaments, familiar yet strange.

She tried them on, for all of us, she claimed, but we knew different—she was re-making acquaintances with long lost friends as we watched and shared her pleasure. There were pendulous domed earrings which draped over her entire ear, sapphire and ruby and pearl sets which transformed her familiar features into those of a mysterious woman, intricately carved bracelets and bangles that covered her entire forearms from wrists to elbows. There were cuffs of filigreed gold that she slipped onto her wrist: connected to the cuff, with fine strands of gold chains, were five rings that fit on the fingers of her right hand. The gold chains connecting the cuff to the rings looked like glittering veins snaking down on the back of her hands. I thought they were elegant and refined.

My sisters, too, tried on some of the ornaments and promises were made to each, accompanied by cries of delight and sorrowful glares, for future trousseaus. The many silver rupees were designated for the future, for elegant coffee and tea services.

My father just nodded as he saw the jewellery. I saw that he had a disinterested look on his face. My brother and I, too, were less interested in the treasures than in the cricket game going on in the nearby field that we were missing. It had been his turn to bat and now he would have lost his place. We were eager to re-join the game and could hear the excited shouts from our gang of neighbourhood kids as ball met bat with heavy thwacks.

But then my attention was drawn back to the box. Underneath all the jewellery boxes lay little packets of white paper, carefully folded. Each packet had writing on it, identifying its contents. These my father opened carefully. In them were gems of all sizes, shapes, and colours. I could see him, for the first time, animated by the new discoveries.

As he opened each packet, he moved the gems inside with his middle finger and told us about them. It turned out that he had a collector's passion for precious and semi-precious gems.

'I have my collection of gems back! Look, these are the opals that I bought in Iran. They are a graduated set. Look how the blue is flecked with green.'

Now I watched the treasures tumbling out of the box with astonishment, as did my brother. In my overheated pre-teen imagination, seeing all this jewellery in a box filled my mind with visions of Errol Flynn, Long John

Silver, and pirates, hunched over a recently dug up treasure chest, as I had seen in movies screened at our high school.

With each new discovery, we were entertained with the piece's story: when my mother got it, who gave it to her, even when she first wore it. Her eyes were twinkling with joy.

'Now I have all my gold jewellery. I won't feel naked again.'

'You feel naked without gold?' I asked incredulously.

'Yes, I do. It's only when I put on gold that I feel that I am fully dressed.'

The last piece to come out of the safe deposit box was a small black velvet pouch with gold-tasselled drawstrings. My mother looked inside the pouch and handed it to my father. 'These, I think, are yours,' she said quite offhandedly, as she passed them on to him.

This was strange, for my father never wore any jewellery. I was finding out new things about him: first that he collected gems, and second, that he had worn and owned jewellery at one time. What else didn't I know, I wondered. He opened the pouch and spilled its contents onto the palm of his left hand. There were, I saw, seven rings, each set with different gems. My father picked out a red ring, looked at it for a length of time, held it up to the light and then quickly gave it to me.

'Here,' he said, 'you keep it. I've given up wearing jewellery. You may like this ruby ring.'

He did not add anything else; no history of where, when, or how he got it. Unlike my mother, who had delighted in giving us the provenance of each piece of her jewellery, he just passed it on to me in an indifferent manner.

If my mother knew of its history, she didn't let on. She just looked on quietly at the transfer.

To a young boy bent on being masculine, a ring, especially a delicate ruby ring, was hardly the embodiment of manliness. While beautiful, it was sexless. Not gorgeous, nor flashy, and not abominably huge like a class ring. My father also gave me a silver ring with a broad, oval jade that lay flat in its setting. On it was carved some writing, in a script which I could not read but which looked like the Urdu script that I had seen in some of his books of poetry.

I took the two rings, muttered a dubious thanks, and promptly gave them to my mother for safekeeping.

Perhaps I should have asked questions about the ruby ring. What was its story? Where did it come from? Where did he get it? Who gave it to him? Why had he stopped wearing jewellery? But, at that young age, and in the societal milieu of the time (where fathers were somewhat aloof and not to be questioned), I did not.

I just accepted his gift quietly.

It was only much later that I unearthed the significance of the ring, and some of the mysteries it held—a lifetime later.

TWO

Jamshedpur, 1950–1960

Jamshedpur was an Edenic place, even though it was the centre of steel-making in India. I was born and brought up there.

As the subcontinent begins to taper into the inverted triangle of the Deccan plateau at its southern end, Jamshedpur is on the Chota Nagpur plateau, at an altitude of 600 feet. It is held in the tight embrace of two rivers in the north-western quadrant of the city: the muddy Kharkai traverses northwards from its source in the Deccan plateau and flows into the Subarnarekha River, the so-called river of gold, at Rivers Meet. From there the enlarged Subarnarekha makes its serpentine way south and east into the Bay of Bengal.

Surrounding the city, and beyond the rivers, are the rolling Dalma hills rising to about 3,000 feet. From everywhere in Jamshedpur, the blue of these hills is a constant and joyous presence. Dense jungles of mahua butter trees, mango and sheesham rosewoods abound, and mother lodes of iron and coal run deep nearby.

Calcutta, the largest city close to Jamshedpur, lies some 150 miles to the east, a metropolis at that time sinking in its own population.

The city of Jamshedpur was also held in a loving embrace and under the paternal vision of the Tata-owned steel company. 'Be sure to lay wide streets planted with shady trees, every other of a quick-growing variety. Be sure that there is plenty of space for lawns and gardens. Reserve large areas for football, hockey, and parks.' Those words of the founder of Jamshedpur were dutifully followed by the town planners.

Growing up in Jamshedpur, surrounded by beautiful and bountiful nature, we did not experience power outages and there was no water rationing. The climate I remember was temperate. All the houses in Jamshedpur were painted regularly by the company. The Tata Main Hospital provided free medical care to all the employees and their families.

My first exposure to the hardships faced by others living in India came when I went to Delhi and other cities at the age of 16, where water and electricity shortages forced residents there to adapt their lifestyles. Relieved of these daily shortcomings, we in Jamshedpur led relatively charmed lives. Compared to other cities, it was also less crowded. The orderly streets, houses, and neighbourhoods were prettier than in any other city.

If, in this enchanting city, you were to leave Rivers Meet, taking the Rivers Meet Road into the city, you would pass Jamshedpur's tiny aerodrome on the right, where propeller planes ferried Tata executives back and forth to Calcutta. The Beldih Club golf course would come up on the right, and if you turned right at the next major intersection on to Bistupur Road, you would pass Loyola High School and its huge expanse of play fields. At the next traffic circle, a left would put you on Straight Mile Road, so-called because it ran for a straight mile to the next big circle at Sakchi market. Straight, until the managing director of the steel plant decided to extend his front lawn, and put in a small traffic circle there, thus placing a slight crimp in that straight mile. Just beyond that hitch in the flow of traffic was the Keenan Stadium on the left, where hockey and football league matches took place, and where the visiting England and West Indies cricket teams matched wits with the state cricket team over five days under a sometimes fierce sun. A right turn at the stadium and then a quick left would put you onto Bagmati Road. If you went down Bagmati for 100 yards or so, down the slope of that road, you would arrive at our bungalow, some two-and-a-half miles from Rivers Meet.

Our house was in the Northern Town area of Jamshedpur, everything in the city being marked off of the location of the steel mill. The entrance to our house was shadowed by a giant peepal sacred fig tree, with its perfectly heart-shaped leaves that rustled and waved in the slightest breeze. Lining our street were colourful gulmohar poinciana trees, which, in their fertile months, lavished the scene with flamboyantly colourful flowers. Off-season, their dried, seeded pods would rattle in the wind.

Our broad street was flanked by two deep, cement-sided drains, like most such roads in Jamshedpur. Our property line was set back by about 20 feet from these drains. At each house, access was provided by a wide entryway over the drains. At the edge of the street, culverts were built over the drains, marking the edges of the access ways, where people could sit and wait for us. I used that culvert to hoist myself on my adult-sized bike when I was ready to learn how to cycle. I remember I promptly fell off the bike and into the drain. Luckily, both of us survived the fall.

Our entryway ended at a dual swing metal gate, which closed shut with a hasp on the top. My brother and I, when we biked back from the school, had perfected a technique to slow-cycle up to the gate, lift the hasp, slip in through the opening, and then, holding one panel of the gate steady with our bike, bring the other panel in and shut the gate. If we did not shut the gate, our mother was quick to send us back to shut it.

The gate was flanked by two tall date palms. A short driveway, with flower beds on both sides and a tall evergreen tree halfway down, took you to the semi-circular veranda on the right, which is where we were sitting that day when the safety deposit box arrived. An old bougainvillea vine shot up one of the pillars holding up the veranda's roof, and its tentacles had spread itself across the top. Purple and pink flowers cheerfully showered down and marked its colourful territory.

Hedges guarded our property on all sides: from the neighbours on the left and right sides and from the street in the front and the alley in the back. On the street side of the veranda was a lawn with flower beds defining its perimeter. An iron swing was built into the far-left end of the lawn. By the swings, and at the hedge line towards the street, was a tall jamun berry tree, almost as high as the peepal tree, which gave up its purply-black juicy fruit all summer long. Because the fruit hung so high, my friends and I would try to bring down a bunch by throwing stones or by using a catapult to shoot them down. What we got, usually, was bruised fruit. What we got, also, were fingers, lips, and tongues stained purple by the fruit. Our clothes would also show the tell-tale stains of the plump berries as we bit into them, or, invariably, as we hurled them at each other. Hanging over our property line, behind the swing, but located in our neighbour's yard, was a guava tree. It gave up its green-hued fruit with crunchy seeded flesh to our marauding hands. When we allowed the fruit to reach its peak, its pale green skin hid a reddish tinged interior that melted like butter in our hungry mouths.

Further, and straight-down the driveway, was a carport, covered with a tin roof, in which my father's black Dodge resided. The back of the carport also marked the end of our property line. Next to the carport, and at the driveway's end, was a gate which let out into the wide back alley between houses on parallel streets. This alley was used by all the tradesmen and the postman on their rounds. At the back gate, also, but on our neighbour's property on the left, was a huge mango tree. This too was marked by us for raiding. Green mangos, ripe mangos, no matter, we ate them all. Quite often the abundant crop of mangos would be given to my mother by the neighbour for her to turn them into a variety of sweet and savoury pickles.

I grew up in this paradise.

My parents and we five siblings lived in that small but comfortable house. The older ones were born in the house.

My eldest sister, who has an eidetic memory, and on whom I have relied heavily for stories about our father and our family as we grew up, still lives in Jamshedpur with her family. She has all the traits ascribed to a first child: reliable, achieving, structured, and controlling. As a child, she had the reputation of being a tomboy and getting into scraps with all and sundry. She is still blunt-spoken but her heart is warm and filled with love and loyalty.

The second oldest sister was the beautiful one in our family. She is affectionate and sincere, fun-loving and I have yet to see her cross.

Our third sister was the quiet one. Of her, it could be said that she ran quiet but deep. If you crossed her, her temper was a quick burn, and you knew to run. Twice I tested her patience, deliberately, and I still carry the scar of stitches on the forehead and on the back of my head as memories of her temper and my stupidity and slowness. Yet she was the one I was closest to. She seemed to take you in, in one glance, and understand you empathetically. Unfortunately, she died of complications arising from rheumatoid arthritis in 1992. She returns often to my dreams and my thoughts.

I am the fourth of the five and the first-born son. If I did not fully understand it then, I do know now, that as the first-born son, I was spoilt by my mother. I was the prince of the house. She provided a base of privilege that, at a subconscious level, imparted a feeling of wellbeing and a cocoon of love. I was the only one, my eldest sister reminds me, who had a special ayah, Lambi Ayah, the tall maid, assigned to me.

Unfortunately, this special treatment afforded me growing up has left me with a sense of entitlement that strays over sometimes, unwittingly, and negatively, into relationships.

I did not question the benefits that my birth order bestowed on me, but I am increasingly sure that it hurt my siblings. I accepted certain givens in my life as a child: that a comfortable house and a good living standard would always be there; that love and the unshakeable bonds with my siblings would be mine; that the fine Jesuit school would be interesting and, at times, a challenge; that my parents would always be together (the notion of divorce was so alien that it never entered my mind); that our home would always be a welcoming place for us no matter what we had done or not done; that we would all have plentiful good food, whenever we wanted it; and, that we would always feel safe and protected.

Because, perhaps, of these subliminal certainties, I was not interested in other matters. I was indolent and lazy, though behind this façade, I was competitive. I was focused, selfishly and indulgently, on enjoyment: playing sports, spending time with my friends, reading, doing easily and passably well in school, and eating.

The youngest of the five is my brother. He is strong as a bull and loyal to a fault. In our frequent wrestling matches, staged and real, he easily bested me. He has always had a large circle of friends. Growing up, he was the one who used to make us laugh a lot with his antics, with his speech, with his rubber face that he could reconstruct into a thousand funny ones. He taught himself how to play the harmonica, and I can still hear the tunes he produced of his own composition.

The five of us, as I remember it, had a good, happy upbringing. We were close, we used to laugh, we used to play pranks.

The easy familial tone was set, no doubt, by my mother, a jovial woman who would patiently help her children with their studies and homework most evenings. From time to time, she would leave us to direct the cook in preparing dinner, check the sauces, add a pinch of this or that, and come back to us. Without missing a beat, she would redirect our attention to the rigors of geometry. Or breathe life into the Mughals' historical exploits, far from their cooler lands in Afghanistan, on the parched and dusty plains of the Ganges. My mother had a graduate degree, and in the early 1930s, had become headmistress of a girl's school in the Punjab, in her small town of Bhaun. That, alone, made her an unusually accomplished and liberated woman in that era.

She was also an excellent cook known all over Jamshedpur for her pickles concocted from mangos, limes, turnips-and-cauliflowers, apples, and gooseberries. We, and especially I, appreciated these accompaniments but for us, and for my father particularly, she was a consummate chef steeped in Sikh and North Indian cuisine. She had a deft hand with spices that would liven up, but never overpower, the meat, lentils, or vegetable she made. And as we completed our homework, or studied for an exam, keen noses were turned to the aromas drifting from the kitchen.

On rare occasions we would go to my father on the veranda for help in physics and chemistry, or he would come by to regale us with tales of his travels into Afghanistan and Iran up to the Silk Road.

But usually he would be comfortably ensconced on the large veranda, immersed in his philosophical pursuits, removed from the day's routines of managing his department, and navigating the organizational politics of the steel plant. His only interest, it seemed to me, and my earliest memory is of him delving into the inner meaning of the Sikh faith.

Sometimes, as he read and wrote, he would hum-sing the poetical shabads, the hymns from the Guru Granth Sahib, the Sikh scriptures. At other times, he would break out in a loud and unmusical, yet pleasing, tarranum singsong and recite Urdu ghazals from the works of Zauq and Iqbal:

Give the gift of sight again, to those who cannot see your wonder
What you have shown me, show them also so they may wonder
Would that my cries arouse each compassionate heart
Would that they would awaken those faint of heart

The set-up on that veranda was specially done to aid him in his writing and reading. He would be seated in a cushioned, cane-bottomed armchair, like a smaller version of a plantation chair. Three tables surrounded his armchair: the one in the front was where he would put up his feet when working, the one on the left held all the books he was reading and the manuscripts he was working on, and the one on the right held a tea service, with a teapot that was constantly kept filled for him by our cook.

In front of him, arrayed in a semicircle, were three more cushioned armchairs, the same as his, for guests, droppersby, or any of us who wished to engage with him.

We called these chairs 'victim's chairs'. My father's wide-ranging mind and interests were focused on philosophy in general and Sikhism in particular. If, by mistake, one of us sat down to ask him about log tables, or the make-up of the earth's crust, or algebra, we would most likely find ourselves, several hours later, listening instead, to the mystical teachings of the Sikh Gurus and the pertinence of their vision to the here and now. While this was diverting and could be entertaining, it was totally inappropriate to Fr Kirsch's chemistry exam at Loyola High the next day, as I found out one time.

I had asked him a simple question. I expected a simple answer. But he took me back to the basics of chemistry before coming to the topic I had asked him about. As the evening stretched into the night, I remember I had complained that I was tired, that it was past my bedtime, that I was sleepy. He simply said, 'You're young. How can you be tired?'

The social set-up in Jamshedpur, at that time, was such that people dropped in to visit with you over a cup of tea at any time they wished. They never called ahead. Many people would arrive at our house between 7 p.m. and 9 p.m. which was when we ate dinner. As my father was a senior manager in the steel company, people were drawn to him for advice. After settling in one of those chairs and with a cup of tea in hand, they might start off with a question about a job opening, or what to do next in a given situation, and hours later, they would be there, in those 'victim's chairs', listening raptly as he expounded on the personality traits of successful people. My father was never one to give you an easy answer, as I had learned to my dismay: he felt the need to train your mind on a vision larger than the next day or the next job.

Around 7 p.m., his part-time typist, Mr Pinto, an Anglo-Indian with a bad stutter, would arrive on his Raleigh bicycle, with his trouser legs correctly clipped away from the messy chain, his tie knotted painfully tight, and, if it were summer, with a pith helmet atop his greying head. His large Adam's apple wobbled with each helplessly caught syllable. He was punctual, erect, meticulous, and transformed my father's beautifully handwritten manuscripts into neatly typed, double-spaced drafts, with four carbons, on a portable Remington Rand. From my workstation at the dining table, I loved to hear the ping, metronomically repeated, each time he turned the lever on the typewriter to advance to the next line.

Somehow that ping also gave substance, even then, to the fact that I grew up in this bubble of stability and love.

THREE

London, 1966–1974

I forgot the ring.

As I went through school and college, it was a case of out of sight, out of mind. Through all those years, it lay, locked up, in the safe of my mother's steel Godrej almirah in my parents' bedroom.

On 14 February 1966, I was about to leave for London to study to become a Chartered Accountant. It was also a time to be given some strange gifts and stranger advice. At Delhi's Palam Airport, the time already past midnight when most flights left India for the west, my father pulled me away from the crowd around us.

'I really like your watch,' he said. 'Could I have it?'

My watch was an inexpensive Indian-made HMT bought, I think, with my first paycheque from a local bank where I worked temporarily as a teller. I loved its wafer-thin, large but elegant dial. I had no idea why he wanted it, nor did I want to part with it.

'You can have my watch in exchange,' he continued.

'But yours is expensive,' I said, eyeing his gold Omega Seamaster.

'Oh, I know. But I like yours. Here, have mine.'

I resisted. This back and forth went on for two more rounds. I was surprised at myself, for I never questioned my father's demands, however circumspectly they were asked.

Around us, Delhi's old Palam Airport was in its usual chaos. Each passenger had a coterie of relatives, friends, and well-wishers who had come to see them off. Screaming children, a long way past their usual bedtime, were throwing tantrums and working out their tiredness on everyone around. Among the crowd were also taxi drivers and porters still bargaining for an extra rupee for their efforts from their impassive clients.

Finally, with a kind, but somewhat exasperated tone signalling the end of negotiations, he said, 'Look, you'll be getting a tiny weekly stipend as an Articled Clerk.'

He was referring to the guild system of becoming a chartered accountant in England: one signed articles of contract with a practicing accountant who provided practical training as well as a small weekly stipend. Over four years, one would work under the accountant while studying on one's own and hopefully pass all three parts of the Institute's exams. I would earn £3 a week, roughly $10 in those days. I was also leaving with $10 in foreign exchange—the maximum allowed by the Government of India. Thus, I knew I would be short of money unless I found a second job. My father, long retired, had already made it clear that he could not support me and that he had no intentions of borrowing money to do so. I was to be on my own.

'If you ever need money in London,' he continued,

'you could pawn off my watch. It's worth something. Yours is pretty much worthless.'

Thus, assured of his confidence in my future success, I gave him my watch in exchange for his chunky and glittery gold one.

But my father was not finished with me. He turned to me and said, 'Remember, London is a large place and you'll be lonely in that big city, even though there will be thousands around you. Keep two things in mind. My mother taught me these and they have helped me negotiate life. First, don't make any fast friends for the first six months. Adopt a wait and see attitude. Get to know people but commit to friendship only once you get to know them well.'

'And the second?' I enquired.

'More important than the first: if you fall in love with anybody, run away. Don't let anything come between you and your work, between you and your destiny.'

My father and I had never discussed sex, let alone love. I remember one night when I was twelve or so. I was in a deep sleep and my parents had just returned from a dinner engagement. My right hand must have been shoved down my pyjama bottoms, perhaps holding on to my penis, for I felt my father remove it. The next morning, he told me that if I ever needed to know anything about sex, I could ask him. I never did. I also remember that several years after that incident, he told me once, out of nowhere, 'A standing penis has no conscience.' I had just looked at him. That was the extent of our talk on love and sex.

Now at the airport, I did not understand his advice

on friendship and love at all but simply nodded. Though I did think to myself, where is this coming from?

Then it was my oldest uncle's turn. 'Our family has a long history of people in high ranks and has a highly-regarded reputation. We come from a prominent clan. Others always talk of us with respect, sometimes with envy. But, we have no money. I have disdained it. Your father has spent most of it freely. Your other uncles are successful but not rich. You make money for yourself and for us.'

This dazed me. My only work experience was of a temporary nature in a bank. I saw myself as others did: a carefree, content, clever but not energetic person. I was also not looking ahead to subsisting on £3 a week, or reaping a fortune out of that.

All I did was nod.

My mother approached me, and I immediately wondered what exchange or advice she had in mind. But all she gave me was a wool blanket made in Ludhiana, by Dhaliwal, a reputable manufacturer of woollen materials. (I think I still have the blanket, hidden deep in some closet of ours.)

'It will be cold in London. I want you to be warm. Take this with you, please.'

Even through its plastic wrapping, I could feel its warmth and its itchy feel. I could not refuse her gift, though I knew I'd look stupid carrying a blanket onto the plane.

She also handed me a small pouch. Inside it was the ring—long forgotten by me but not by her. It lay there, looking up at me, its rubypink eye wondering, perhaps.

'It's your father's gift. Keep it safe and with you always. Now you may want to wear it,' she said.

I was just shy of my 22nd birthday. Since then, I've worn the ring daily. Living as I did in bedsitters or student housing in England, there would be no safe places where I could easily store the ring. I kept everything of value, except my passport, with me always. I had also fallen under the cabochon ruby ring's hypnotic spell. Deep down I believed that there was a story attached to it. My father had not been forthcoming that day he gave it to me. But, I had a gnawing feeling that there was more. The ring was still exquisite and still sexless. However, its elegance, its artistic cohesiveness spoke of taste. Where did he get this and why did he have it? These were questions that surfaced in my mind from time to time but more present and pressing matters always quashed these thoughts.

I had no inkling that the ring held hidden connotations. I was, also, just not curious. I had something my father gave me, and I liked the way the gold sparkle of the Omega on my left wrist complemented the ring on the right hand. I did not have any need to know more about the origins of the ring.

In any case, as fate would have it, I would only have two chances to find out anything about it from him directly.

I visited India twice between 1966 and 1974. Both times, I was there for two short weeks—the extent of my annual vacation (and a reflection on the paucity of my savings). On neither occasion did I get to talk to my parents, especially to my father, about the ring, especially since I had no idea that it had a hidden past.

The first time, in December 1970, I went back to get married to a French woman I had met in London.

My mother was wildly happy but, nonetheless, chided me good-naturedly saying she had missed out on a lot of jewellery which had been offered to her by parents of Sikh girls who wanted their daughter to be married into our family. In fact, she had kept a running score of the number of times she had been approached, and even wrote to me, in London, about some of them. My advice, somewhat facetious, was that she should readily accept the money and jewels and then blame me for being stubborn in refusing to meet the girl. She knew, and I knew, that deep down my parents wanted me to make my own choice.

The marriage preparations alone had her in a tizzy. The moment we arrived, my mother whisked my fiancée away for fittings, to purchase jewellery, to the sari shops and a hundred other things. My father, who was a methodical organizer was, meanwhile, busy in making sure the wedding would go off well.

The few private moments that my parents and I had were spent discussing my job in London (I had recently completed my Articles and had joined Arthur Andersen, one of the Big 8 accounting firms at that time), about my living conditions (we lived in a lovely flat in Holland Park in London overlooking a private community garden), about her parents and family, and about my future ambitions.

At the end of our visit, my parents took us to the railway station to see us off to Calcutta, from where we would go back to London via Delhi. I remember standing in the open doorway of the compartment as the coal-fired train chug-chugged its way out of Jamshedpur, its wheels slipping, and then getting traction on the rails as it gained speed. My father was standing on the platform looking at me and, as his frame became smaller and smaller, I wondered if I would see him again. He was seventy-one and I was twenty-six.

I saw him once again on my next visit to India in January 1974. This time I was alone and had gone to India with the idea of finding a job there and moving back. I had a few interviews lined up with large corporations and some more contacts to follow up on. My parents were not happy and sat me down in the drawing room in our house in Jamshedpur. My father asked me why I wanted to work in India and then forestalled my answer by asking if it was because I would be nearer to them. I said, yes, as indeed that was part of my reasoning.

'Look,' my father said, 'I am seventy-five and I feel strong. I can take care of your mother and myself and don't want you to come back simply because you may be called upon to take care of us.'

'By the way,' he added, 'it takes you about 36 hours to get to us from London via Calcutta and the Steel Express train. It will take you about 7 to 8 hours to get to us from Bombay by air if you take this job. Or 36 hours, if you come by train. So, please don't bother about a job in India.'

Then he said something strange that still resonates with me. 'Listen,' he said, 'as I told you, I am strong now. But there will come a time when your mother and I will get weaker, when we will need help, and at that time, she, and maybe I, will write to you to come back to help us. Listen to me while I am strong: I want you to tear up those letters; I don't want you to listen to our pleas. We will do everything we can to "blackmail you emotionally" but I want you to shut your mind and your heart to it.'

I was absolutely dumbfounded. I couldn't believe what he was saying. I looked at my mother and she was smiling and said, 'Yes, that's right, Gudoo.' ('Little doll' was my nickname from when I was a child, and was one I detested; she was the only person who could call me that and she used it very sparingly knowing of my dislike.)

'We don't want to hold you back,' she said. 'You go out and scale the heights you were meant to, without fear,' she added. I was in tears; as I am, again, in writing this.

Well, you can imagine my emotional state over the next few days that I spent with them.

The topic of the ring did not come up that time either.

Thus, I never did learn about the ring until long after my parents died, quite suddenly, eight months later at the end of the summer in 1974.

FOUR

Jamshedpur, August–September 1974

A telegram pushed through the mail slot of my flat in London announced my mother's passing.

I had just come back from work that Thursday. With me was a restaurateur friend who owned an Indian restaurant in Southall, a hub for Asian immigrants on the western outskirts of London. He had come home with me for tea and a chat. But when he saw the telegram and saw my reaction, he quietly led me to the living room where I collapsed on the sofa. We talked for a while about her, and then he left.

At age sixty, my mother had died, prematurely, of a stroke on 29 August 1974. 'Come when you can', my father wrote in the telegram. The cremation usually takes place the same day, or at most, the day after a person dies. The body, it is held, has completed its function of housing the soul temporarily: there is no longer any need for it. The soul has transmigrated and merged with its Maker: judgment, which is immediate and personal, has been passed and the body returned to its foundational dust.

Lines from Kabir, the mystical Sufi philosopher-poet in fifteenth-century India, rote memorized and studied in high school, flitted through my head, as I imagined her cremation.

'Carefully, Brother,' the clay says to the potter,

> *'Why do you dig me up so hurtfully?*
> *Don't you know that a day will come?*
> *When I will bury you eternally?'*
> *'Carefully, Brother,' the tree says to the carpenter*
> *'Why do you cut me down so painfully?*
> *Don't you know that a day will come?*
> *When I will burn you agonizingly?'*

'Come when you can' meant we will have cremated your mother but come for the services celebrating her life.

I did go, reaching home on the seventh day after her passing. The journey took two days from London, via Calcutta and a train from there to Jamshedpur. I had also tracked down my brother to a beach town in Italy where he was vacationing with his girlfriend. He hadn't left any addresses or contacts when he left London. Finally, in desperation, I called a radio station in Portofino, Italy, where his girlfriend was from, and persuaded them to air messages asking him to contact me. A friend of his who heard the messages gave me the number to his hotel. I reached him at two in the morning to tell him the sad news and we agreed that he would return to London and catch a flight the next day. He would arrive a day after I did in Jamshedpur.

When I reached home, it was around midnight. My father met me at the door and hugged me fiercely.

Tears were streaming freely down his cheeks. Even when he was asking me about the details of my journey, the tears continued. There were no catches in his throat, no impediment to his speech, no convulsive sobs, but the tears continued, unbidden.

He took me to the drawing room and brought out a jar. 'These,' he said, with a catch in his voice, 'are your mother's flowers.' That is how we Sikhs refer to cremains. I looked at the jar and her cremains, my reactions numbed by my tiredness and fatigue.

My brother-in-law and my oldest sister were there in the house and we sat down to have some tea and talk, even though it was well past midnight, and even though I was beyond exhaustion. My sister related to me the circumstances of my mother's death. This is a typical Indian custom, of retelling the circumstances leading to a person's demise, and is related to most who come to mourn. There is something in that ritual of sharing that informs and reduces the pain at the same time.

'She was resting comfortably when we left her that last night,' she said.

'Yes, but remember what Papaji said,' my brother-in-law interjected referring to my father, 'we had to make sure that she survived the dawn because that's when most stroke patients pass.'

My father meanwhile was asking me if I was hungry and needed something else to eat. He coaxed me into trying some of the savoury snacks my mother had made just a few days earlier. The tears still streamed down his face.

Tired after my long journey, I told him I wanted to sleep.

'You have your entire life ahead to sleep,' my father said. 'Tonight, I want to talk to you.' Indeed, in my room, we lay on two beds side by side, and he talked through the entire night. When I fell asleep around eight in the morning, he left my room and went out to manage more of the preparations. That next night my brother arrived and, again, my father insisted on speaking to both of us through the night. Again, he busied himself with supervising the next morning and day.

He spoke of many things and of nothing, those nights. It was a stream-of-consciousness unburdening of his life with my mother, of his family, of her family, of lessons he had learned from life, of his hopes for all of us, on advice on how to conduct our lives, and more. At one point, he said, he had hoped to have written down all the crossroads he had come upon in his life. All the major problems and how he had solved them. What had worked and what had not. 'You too,' he said, 'will come on these same junctions. The circumstances will be different, but the problems will be the same.'

'Wouldn't it be wonderful, he said, 'if I could tell you how I navigated through the crossroads, so you wouldn't have to learn it for yourself again?'

In my sleepy state, I thought that was a novel but an untenable idea. Years later, I read that, when Alexander Solzhenitsyn left Russia to settle in the US, he wrote an open letter to the American people. In that, he said that we were making the same mistakes that the Soviet Union had made. What if, he told us, he could relay those Soviet mistakes to us and how the Soviet Union, in hindsight, should have resolved them: could we not benefit from their experience? And, in answer to his rhetorical question, he acknowledged that the human ego was such that we could not countenance anyone else having the same problems as we did. Thus, as Otto von Bismarck said, 'fools learn from experience'.

Through my job, then at a merchant bank in London, I had some experience with computers used by banks, and it seemed to me that my father's stream-of-consciousness talk was like an off-line back-up of precious files, to ensure that they were not lost if the mainframe crashed.

~

My mother came from an influential, politically prominent family. Her father was the political agent of the North-West Frontier States Agency in British-ruled pre-partitioned India, equivalent, somewhat, to the vice governor of the region. He reported to the British head of the Agency. His charge was to use political means to pacify the indigenous Pathans in the region where British military might had failed.

My mother grew up in a large two-storeyed house in Bhaun, where, reportedly, her father maintained the wherewithal to house and feed up to 100 needy people at any given time.

When my parents got married, my father and his family and friends went to her town for the marriage. There were 200 of them in his *junj*, the groom's party, and they were to be hosted—lodged, feted, and entertained—for about a week as is typical of Sikh weddings. Most of them stayed in her father's house.

On the ground floor there was a special section for the family's five horse carriages. All the horses and other livestock were stabled there as well. Our mother told us once that the reception for their wedding was held on the large, flat roof. All 200 of them and her extended family were seated at long tables. New chairs had been specially commissioned for that occasion. The night before, my mother heard noises of birds chattering and the flapping of wings coming from the roof. She went up and discovered a large cage in one section of the roof. Inside it were hundreds of partridges and quails that would be served as one of the courses for one of the dinners. She could not countenance the killing of living things just for her marriage. She opened the cage and set them free. Her act of defiance and piety notwithstanding, the next day hundreds more birds were brought in for the dinner.

My mother was short, not even 5 feet tall, slightly overweight, and always dressed elegantly in a sari. These were not ostentatious, but artistically tasteful. She always wore a lot of jewellery—earrings, a necklace, and lots of bangles on her wrist. Always a matched set, these would also complement the sari she was wearing. She had a dazzling smile and laughed freely and often. Her gaze was always straightforward, her expression open and guileless. She had no hidden agendas, and she did not shy from speaking plainly. Kids loved her because she could laugh and play as one of them; adults loved her because she was intelligent and fun to be with. Our neighbourhood had many different communities: our immediate neighbours were Bengalis, Punjabis, Parsis, South Indians, Anglo-

Indians, Biharis. We knew them all. My mother formed deep relationships with all the neighbouring mothers. Quite often, after lunch was over, they would gather together on our veranda or in our inner courtyard. Sometimes, in the winter months, they would bring bags of peas and all the women, seated on chairs or on mooras, the woven stools, would help in shelling them while they chatted. I could hear my mother's voice telling stories, and peals of laughter from the assemblage. We also had a tandoor in our inner courtyard, and I have a lovely image of my mother with two of the neighbourhood ladies making tandoori rotis, all of them laughing at something my mother had said.

She was a strong person with strongly held principles and faith, who led by example and was a patient teacher. Her striking and attractive personality commanded attention in any room she was in. She always carried out her commitments with dignity. Her friends were loyal to her. Long after she was gone, many of them kept in touch with us and made sure that we did not feel her loss too acutely.

She was indomitable. Once, when my sisters were late returning from the nearby Sacred Heart Convent School, my mother sent our gardener to find out what was keeping them. We were all waiting to eat lunch with them. My father had already gone back to the office. The gardener came back, running, and alarmed. It seemed that rowdy hordes of boys from another school in town had decided, on some made-up pretext, that they wanted to shut down their school as well as all the others in the city. They were surrounding the Sacred Heart Convent

School and not allowing anyone to leave unless the Sisters of Mercy who ran the school, promised to shut down the school for the next few days. There was a standoff with fearful children locked inside the school gates and anxious nuns not knowing what to do. Outside, the crowd of boys were hurling taunts at the students and generally working themselves up to a frenzy.

Mother left us at the lunch table and strode over to the school. She saw a boulder near the front gate. As my sisters and their friends anxiously looked out at the jeering boys, my mother, with the help of some other parents who were just standing around not knowing what to do, got up on the boulder and harangued the crowds. 'Shame on you,' she said, 'these are your sisters. You should protect them and take care of them. But look at you. You're worthless and shameless. You're trying to harm them. Go home to your mothers.'

Within a few minutes, the boys slunk away cowed by her spirit. My sisters later reported that they were horrified and embarrassed by her actions. But she rescued them.

Above all, she is remembered as being funny and being the first to laugh at her own mistakes and foibles. One night she was carrying all the crockery for dinner to the dining room from the kitchen where they were stored. Seven dinner plates, seven side plates, and seven bowls, all stacked one on the other. It had rained that day, and the semi-circular veranda that ran along the open inner courtyard and which linked the kitchen to the dining room, was a little slick. She slipped and fell. When we all hurried over to her hearing the noise, she was sitting on the floor, amidst the shards of broken china and laughing. Tears of laughter were streaming down her face. We all burst out laughing, too, and my father joined in as well. In between her laughing spells, she said that we, the children, made her tense. She good-naturedly used to call us *khasma nu khaniyo marjanyo*: just an endearing way to say to all of us that we caused her so much trouble. Also, she would add for good measure to us brothers, *aafat de partaalyo,* mischief-makers.

It was a good dinner we had that night. And a new dinner service arrived the next day.

I remember my mother as an easy-going person but one who had a will of steel. I came up against this on one occasion while was I going to college in Jamshedpur. Every evening, my friends and I would engage in an aimless promenade on the main street of the Bistupur market. One evening we had gone to visit a classmate in her house on the outskirts of the city. We had cycled there and, on the way back, around 10 p.m., had ducked into a roadside tea stall for refreshments. The stall serviced coolies and was in a poor section of the city. It was mostly a slum. I knew that my mother would not approve, especially since my father was on his consulting job in a nearby town. I thought I was hidden well in the depths of the stall. We were sitting there having tea when my mother, by coincidence, happened to drive past the stall. I was surprised because she never went to that part of the town. She caught sight of me and told the driver to bring me to the car. I went out and found her sitting in the back seat looking at me quite sharply. She had a disgusted look on her face.

'Don't bother coming home tonight,' she said. Then

she motioned for the driver to continue. I finally biked back home, arriving around 11 p.m. It was a cold January night, but when I got to the back patio, I saw that all the doors were locked. My mother was standing inside the house, looking out of the large, barred window. She told me, 'You've disgraced your father by drinking tea in that slum. Don't you know your father's position in the town? You have brought down his prestige by what you did.'

I protested. 'It was just tea. There was no shame in this,' I said. 'Let me in,' I said, 'I'm shivering.'

But my mother just turned her back and said go back to your friends in the tea stall. Undaunted, I dragged out a string bed that was in the corner of the patio, took off my turban, wrapped it around me and lay on the bed, defiantly. But I was shivering uncontrollably because of the cold.

At 2 a.m., I got up from my fitful sleep. I was cold through to my bones. I walked over to the window and my mother was still there, standing, looking out at me. 'Had enough?' she enquired.

Not to be outdone I said, 'no, have you had enough?'

At this, both of us burst out laughing and she let me in. 'Remember,' she said, 'don't do this again. Your father's prestige depends on all our actions, not just his.'

Prestige. I would come across that again.

My father would always bring my mother gifts on her birthday and on their anniversary. Often, he would break off a flower from the many rose bushes in the garden and present it to her. Later, in the 1970s, when he did not have a car and was almost blind with cataracts, he would walk to the Bistupur market, a mile away, and bring back small gifts for her. Just because...

When my mother died, my sister told me later, and her body was brought back home, she was bathed as is our custom, and then her body was dressed as a bride's because she had preceded her husband in death. The front bedroom of our house had been cleared of furniture and she was lying on the ground, in keeping with Sikh tradition. Friends and mourners crowded into the room and sat on the floor keeping a vigil until her body would be taken to the cremation grounds. My father was sitting next to my sister and her husband. He was crying. He said: 'Look at me, a seventy-five-year-old man crying for a sixty-year-old woman.' Then, he said to my sister, 'Look at your mother. She is dead, but she is still the prettiest woman in this room.'

My maternal grandfather was not a Sikh though he had married a Sikh woman. At the time my mother married my father, arranged marriages were based on clan relationships and not on religion. Sikhs were held in high regard by the surrounding population and the tradition in the Punjab was that the oldest daughter or son from a Hindu family would marry into a Sikh family. This was what happened with my mother. My mother's names were apt: her unmarried name was Vidya or wisdom; her married Sikh name was Kanchan or gold.

She loved us fiercely, and we responded equally.

In keeping with Sikh traditions, on the eleventh day after my mother's death a non-stop, round-the-clock reading of the Guru Granth Sahib, the Sikh scriptures, was undertaken by a relay of readers. The Akhand Path, or 'unbroken prayer', is an uninterrupted recitation. The final ritual would take place on the thirteenth day after her passing.

Each evening, leading up to the beginning of the Akhand Path, a Sikh granthi came to our house to sing hymns from the Guru Granth Sahib. While Sikhs don't have a priestly class, we do have people who are knowledgeable in its teachings, hence granthi, and who are also trained to sing its hymns in the classical Indian tradition of ragas prescribed to each hymn.

'Sing only songs of joy and praise for she was a special woman, and we have much to praise about her,' my father had instructed Bhai Isher Singh, the granthi. My father was hyperactive in the way he organized every aspect of my mother's service. After her death, as I was told by my eldest sister who lived in Jamshedpur, he planned the entire service, sent out invitations, thought out the lunch details, and had the entire interior of the house cleaned from top to bottom, quite often helping in the process. The garden had been carefully cleaned up as well, the lawn was mowed, and the flower beds tidied. He wanted to make sure that whoever came to 'her house' found it to be in the condition she always kept it. After spending the whole day in physical activity, he wouldn't, or couldn't, sleep.

~

I think that was the first time I realized how deeply he loved my mother. In the 1950s and 1960s, when I grew up, there wasn't much in the way of public affection that Indian parents displayed. The only time I can recall him showing his feelings was in the late 1950s when my eldest sister got married. My mother had always been prone to low blood pressure and palpitations of the heart, and after the week-long ceremonies had ended and my sister had left on her honeymoon, I came back from a pick-up game of cricket to find her in bed with my father sitting next to her. His hand was under the quilt and he was slowly massaging her chest. 'She's having palpitations and I'm trying to get her to relax a little. She'll be all right. I'm here. I'm with her.'

I remember being astonished by his assertion. He was there, and he would protect her.

Thinking back, I remembered one other occasion where he showed how much he loved her. It was in January 1974, when I was visiting Jamshedpur. My mother was dressed up and leaving for a luncheon party. My father rarely went out and hated social events. But she loved parties and crowds. So, she would go alone. She always told us that she had to keep up our high social standing in the town, our prestige. Again, that notion.

When my mother went out, she would put on a dab of perfume, apply lipstick and, if it was during the day, she would put on fashionable dark glasses, upturned at the corners. They were so dark we used to tease her that she was 'going incognito'.

My father and I were sitting on the veranda that late morning, and, as my mother got into the car to be driven away, he turned to me and said: 'Every time your mother gets dressed up like that to go out, I feel jealous.' I was shocked not only by the naked truth of that statement but also that he found my mother so fetching.

I came to a deeper realization of my father's loneliness twelve days after my mother's passing. He had spent all that time preparing for her final service and he'd spent the previous nights talking to my brother and me, nonstop. Physically, he was spent. But he was a tough person and built to not show his emotions openly. Somewhere though, under his armour, he came to realize that he would be alone without her. All his life, he had leaned on her for social interaction, disdaining the company of other people. But she was always at his side, and now she wasn't. This realization must have struck him hard. He was not prepared to leave the house that he had built for her and for himself. I had suggested that he come and live with me in London, but he had quickly brushed off that idea. Truth be told, I couldn't see him confined in my small flat in London that could easily fit in the kitchen of his house. He wasn't prepared either, to live at my sister's house which was just a ten-minute walk away from his. He was a territorial man and was neither able nor willing to give up his domain. In addition, he must have been cognizant of the tradition of not spending a night in your daughter's married home: her home being her husband's and not hers. As the reality of my mother's death and his aloneness sank in, I think he was shaken to his core. While he did not show it, stoic as he was, I sensed his struggle.

On the last day, just as my mother's services were about to end, my father passed away.

After a night talking with us, he had got up early to continue his supervision of preparations for my mother's service: a large crowd was expected. He had had his usual large breakfast of two paranthas and scrambled eggs. Around 10:30, he felt restless and went to lie down. I was seated beside his bed and he asked me to read him the letters of condolence that had poured in. He was twisting and shifting uncomfortably in bed.

'Is everything all right?' I asked. 'You don't seem to be too comfortable.'

He just smiled wanly at me and said: 'I'm fine. Go on reading.'

But I could see that he was not all right. He kept changing his position in bed. Outside, more relatives, from my mother's side, had arrived. Her side of the family was well known for its loud gregariousness; they assembled, from far and wide, whenever there was a momentous occasion. Usually, this was a wedding or a birth.

Now death had struck their oldest sister, and here they were. In their family, it was customary to show grief by wailing. It was, however, foreign to my father and his side of the family, and it was forbidden under Sikh custom. Their loud wails of mourning were unsettling to him; I could see that. I went outside and asked them to quiet down which, thankfully, they did. Inside, though, his restlessness continued.

I asked him several times if I should call the doctor, but he maintained that he was fine.

'I need a bedpan,' he said. 'Can you get me one and help me?' He directed me to the mezzanine attic in our house. He had had that built as a storage area in the house. Concrete shelves ran the length of the attic.

'You have to stoop to go in, as the ceiling there is only 4 feet high. Go into the inner room of the attic, which is just above this bedroom. In the right-hand corner, on the shelf, you'll find a bedpan. It's on the second shelf from the top.'

His unease continued, and eventually I asked my eldest sister to call the doctor. The doctor, his friend, came immediately, and after checking his vital signs, asked him: 'What is the matter? All your indications are good, but your pulse is weakening.'

'Doctor,' he said, 'I don't want to live anymore.'

I was dazed by this bald statement from a man who just nine months earlier had declared that he felt fit and strong.

At the doctor's insistence, we took him to the Tata Main Hospital. On the way to the hospital, in the ambulance, I sat next to him. His eyes were closed. As the ambulance made its final turn to the hospital, he opened his eyes and looked at me, piercingly, just once, as if to say: 'Goodbye. Good luck.' He died before the doctors could see him.

It was 12:30 p.m. on 9 September 1974.

Later that day, we took him to the cremation grounds in Jamshedpur on the banks of the Kharkai River. As is the custom, as the eldest son, I lit his funeral pyre. I asked my brother to help me. On our return to the house, a crowd of mourners had collected. One of them, an old family friend of ours and a Sikh, came forward and gave me a new white turban. It was his way of acknowledging that I, as the eldest son, had now become the head of the family.

My father was seventy-five. I was thirty and orphaned.

An eerie emptiness inhabited the house after my parents' deaths. Before I left for London, I went up to his library. All the books had been donated—my father's manuscripts, copies of his own books, and other files were all that was left. I leafed through them and took as much as I could stuff into my suitcase. The rest I left behind at my sister's home and brought back on later trips.

One such file contained all the letters he had written home to his family from America while he lived there in the 1920s. He had also collected all the letters I had written home to him and to my mother from London. He had kept copies of the letters he had written me. In that one folder, there was a lot of information that I would find handy later.

It was interesting, too, to compare his writings to his family, and the tone of those letters, to those that I had written. We were both in our early 20s: His letters were intellectual and showed a keen mind trying to comprehend spirituality and the physical conditions around him, while mine were mostly prosaic musings on the news and the minutiae of my everyday life.

Back in London after the services, I opened the door to my flat and looked at all the accumulated mail, pushed through the mail slot, lying on the floor. When later I went through the pile, I was amazed to find a letter from my mother.

The letter had been written a day before she passed away. It had been mailed that day, arriving while I was in India attending her funeral services.

My mother had written a short message in the aerogramme: that a mother's duty is to educate her son, feed him well, and keep him healthy. The rest, she wrote, is up to God.

To me, it was a message from beyond and her way of saying farewell: She had done her job well and the rest was up to me and God.

I wept uncontrollably for the first time since my parents' passing.

FIVE

Alexandria, Virginia, 1981

The death of my parents within days of each other had removed the last link to the ring. Then serendipity intervened. A chance remark by one of my uncles in the early 1980s started my journey to learn more about the ring. My uncle, number four out of the nine siblings, and his wife were visiting me in DC where I had moved from London. By now, I was divorced and alone.

During a nostalgic evening of do-you-remember and did-you-know, my uncle and aunt, at my prompting, told me about my father's early life in Quetta. Much of this was unknown to me, partly because my father never spoke about himself.

'Your father wasn't always bookish like you remember him. No, not at all: he was handsome and charismatic, engaging, and friendly,' my uncle told me. 'He had a large group of friends and inspired a great deal of loyalty from them. He was quite a catch and sought after by parents with marriageable daughters,' my uncle added.

'Did you get that from your father?' he queried, pointing at my ruby ring.

'Yes, he gave it to me when I was quite young,' I replied, totally nonplussed about where this was going.

He then asked what I knew about the ring. I shrugged and told him I knew very little.

My uncle then proceeded to fill me in with his knowledge of the ring and its history. 'Your father met a woman in America, and they had a passionate love affair. Did you know that?'

This was the first time I'd heard about this. I was stunned.

'So, this was before he was married? Was she married? You called it an affair.'

'I'm not sure, but I think she was not married. He came back from the States in 1928, I believe. He didn't get married until 1937, almost ten years later.'

He didn't have any more details about the woman in America, not even about how and where my father had met her. But she was the person who gave him the ring, my uncle said.

'Here's what I know,' he went on. 'When my brother left America to return to Quetta in 1928, the woman, whose name I do not remember, had calculated that the journey home to Quetta, by boat and train, would take him forty days. She gave him a packet of forty letters. She also gave him that ring you are wearing.'

'After he reached Quetta,' my uncle continued, 'he used to get daily letters from her which he meticulously kept in a large, locked trunk in his room. The letters were long and came regularly for about three years. He told us he never responded. Then, when he finally wrote to her, the letters ceased.'

My first reaction to this bit of news was shock. I never imagined that my father would be romantically involved with anyone other than my mother, and even there he showed no outward signs of affection for her. Then all the other questions came flooding in: Did my mother know? Had he told her of his past love affair when they got married? How had it ended? Why did it end? I wondered, too, what had happened to the letters: Did any of them survive? If so, who had them?

Then my uncle astonished me even further by telling me the following story. He had heard this second hand from yet another uncle of mine who lived in Delhi.

'In 1967, an American man arrived in Delhi. He met your parents and your middle sister Kiran in a hotel in Delhi. He claimed to be the son of the American woman.'

'Was my father his father?'

'That I don't know.'

My first reaction on hearing this story was that it was nonsense. But, in later years, the story of the man claiming to be her son was confirmed by two other uncles who lived in Delhi at the time of this encounter.

When I later talked to my sister, who did not recall much of the meeting, I asked her, 'What was his name? Surely you remember that?'

'I'm not sure,' she said, 'but it sounded like Cary or Gary.'

She could not add much to my uncle's story. But she did say that she had seen some of the letters among our father's books in his library. 'I know my daughter saw them. She was nine or so, and she had discovered a bunch of letters in his study. She used to try to read them but couldn't.'

Suddenly I was determined to find out more. The ring now had a story and a past, though one that was fraught with danger. Did I want to find out more about the woman? Did I have a half-brother somewhere? Then there were the letters. If my sister had seen them, why hadn't she told me about them? Where were they now, and who had them?

The more I thought about it, the more fascinating the mystery became. And I loved solving problems.

This was a more personal knot to unravel. But for another long period of time, life intervened and the mystery of the ring remained untouched. I forgot about the whole thing.

SIX

New Delhi, December 1987

When I entered the large ballroom of the many-starred luxury hotel in New Delhi, it was to the iconic drumbeat of the bhangra. Under the influence of Sikh-British DJs, its shoulder-jiggling, finger-snapping, toe-tapping rhythms had been remixed, and the energetic folk dance of the Sikhs had become an internationally recognized dance style.

It was December 1987, and I was at the wedding reception for my niece, the daughter of my eldest sister. I had arrived several days into the many rituals and parties that surround a Sikh wedding. My niece was resplendent in a red sari with gold zari embroidery and, as always with a Sikh bride, she was covered in heavy gold jewellery. Her hands were hennaed in intricate patterns and, I imagined, her feet as well. Down the parting of her hair, there was a faint streak of reddish-orange sindoor powder signifying that she was married. While this is not traditional among Sikhs, I figured she was wearing it as a fashion statement.

As I looked at her, I saw the young baby with huge eyes who used to crawl over to me wanting to be picked up. I could still picture her, at two, clambering up the stairs to my room and taking hold of my hand to bring me down to the dining table for lunch or dinner. Now, at twenty-four, she was a beautiful, self-confident adult.

It was a cold Delhi evening where the damp seeps deep into your bones, but my niece had just wandered off the dance floor after a half an hour of frenetic dancing. Slightly out of breath, she spotted me and came forward to hug me. My hands were outstretched as well. My niece grabbed hold of my hand and took a closer look at the ring I was wearing.

'What a pretty ring you have! I saw it immediately. Where did you get it?'

'I got it from...'

'Wait, is this the ring your father gave you? The one that the woman—you know, his girlfriend in America—gave him? I never saw it before. But my mother told me about it and how your father gave it to you.'

'Well, yes, this is the one,' I began.

'I knew it! I knew it! You know, I have a secret to confess to you: I have a packet of letters his girlfriend wrote him. I kept them! Nobody knows but, of course, you do now.'

I was dumbstruck. So, the letters had survived. How many, I did not know. But I immediately knew that I had to get them.

'You have the letters?'

'Not all of them, but I think I have 30 or 40...'

'How did you get them? I need to see them.'

'Grandfather gave them to me. I was an inquisitive child, and I often used to sit in his study while he was there and explore all the books on the shelves. Sometimes he made me read from the books. He also made me read his manuscripts. As you know, he was quite blind by then.'

I just nodded, eager to hear more about the letters.

'One day, I found these letters and asked him about them. He didn't say anything, so I started reading them, but I couldn't. The writing was difficult to read, it was slanted way over to the left. Anyway, one day I asked him if I could keep them, and he said yes. So, I have them.'

'You have them here in Delhi?'

'Yes of course I have them here. Where else would I keep them? You've read them, haven't you?'

'No, I haven't. I didn't even know they existed. My uncle mentioned some letters a few years ago, but I thought they had all been destroyed or lost during Partition.'

Meanwhile, my mind was racing. Once the initial shock wore off, I knew I had to get them from her and quickly as I was leaving in a few days to go back to Washington, DC. Until that moment, I hadn't known the letters still existed. I had to have them!

'Look,' I said, 'I know you've been very busy this week…'

Once again, she cut me off. 'Not only this week but for months, Mamaji.'

'Just this week there were seven events. I must run. I can see my mother-in-law waving to me. I have to get back to my throne.'

She made a move to go to a raised dais at one end of the ballroom with two ornate chairs under an even more ornate canopy. There, the couple were supposed to sit, like royalty, and wait for well-wishers to come up and offer their heartfelt wishes for a long, married life.

'Listen,' I said, putting a restraining hand on her, 'it's important that I talk to you about these letters. I know you're in a rush right now. How about lunch tomorrow? Can you make it to the Bukhara at one?'

She grinned and said: 'Wow, Bukhara! We'll be there, but don't blame me if we're a little late.'

At Bukhara the next day, deep in the bowels of the ITC Maurya, there was no sign of the newlyweds. It was well after 1 p.m., and the waiter had filled my water glass several times before enticing me to order a glass of chilled Kingfisher beer. My fellow Articled Clerk, at the firm of accountants in London where we had both served our accounting apprenticeships, happened to be the managing director of the hotel's parent company. He had instantly arranged a table when I'd called him earlier that morning and had come by to chat for a few minutes, calling over the maître d' to tell him I was to be given VIP service.

The place exuded elegance as befitted a much sought-after restaurant in an exclusive hotel. The menu was from the north-western region of pre-partition India and reflected its origins. A few diners I knew had come over to congratulate me on my niece's wedding, and some had invited me to join them while I waited. But I wanted to be alone.

My mind was still in a whirl: all night long, I had tussled with the bedsheets. Who was this mystery woman? What was she like? Where, and how, had my father met her? My father the object of such desire? No, I couldn't believe it. Did he return her passion? If he had, who was this father I did not know? Why had he deliberately withheld that side of himself from us?

That night in Delhi, after the wedding, I had finally fallen asleep around dawn and woken, groggily, around noon. The taste of ersatz scotch furred my tongue and no amount of masala tea seemed able to remove it. After I called my friend, the MD, and was assured I could come at any time and that a table would be waiting, I showered, lingering in the cold spray, and hurried out to a catch a taxi to the restaurant. And here I was waiting.

Unconsciously, I had been twirling the ring. Now I studied it. I decided that, after a long period of wearing the ring without knowing its origins, I would not give up until I had put flesh and blood on this woman who had given the ring to my father, and learned the facts of their romance.

~

'Ah, there you are!' My niece, with her new husband in tow, had finally arrived. Though it was 2:30, there wasn't a single note of apology for their lateness. It was, after all, the land of IST: Indian Stretchable Time.

'My, I'm hungry, Mamaji. You've eaten, haven't you? Oh, no, why didn't you order? WAITER!' The waiter appeared as if by magic and took our orders: raan, malai kebabs, lamb chops, daal, a couple of vegetables, raita with cucumber and, of course, a table-sized garlic naan; all to be washed down with salt-and-pepper lassi and more beer.

I'd had enough of the delay and wanted to get to the matter at hand. 'Look,' I said to my niece just as she was about to start chattering, 'tell me where you have the letters and when you can give them to me.'

'But Mamaji, they're mine. Grandfather let me have them, and I've preserved them. Besides, they are so sentimental and are of such emotional value to me. But I can give you copies if you like.'

'No,' I said firmly, 'I want the originals. I'll make copies for you. Where are they, and when can I get them?' I was being unusually blunt, but the idea of holding a piece of paper that *she* had written on and that *he* had read spurred me on. I was counting, too, on the very Indian notion of respecting one's elders.

We spent the next hour or so arguing back and forth. My niece was reluctant to give them to me, and I was adamant about getting them.

'But why do you want them?' she asked.

'I want to get to the bottom of this,' I said. 'I want to find out who this woman was.'

'But why Mamaji?' she countered, 'I'm sure she's dead. Your father is dead. Why dig it up? Why do you want to delve into his very private life? Won't it be painful for you and your siblings?'

'No,' I said, showing her the ring. 'My father gave this to me, and I think he had a purpose. He wanted me to find out about her and who she was. Beyond that, I think he wanted me to discover him as well.'

After the kulfi and rabri desserts and elaichi tea, my niece said, 'Okay, I'll give them to you. I have them at home, and if you come by tomorrow, I'll dig them out.'

Satisfied, I leaned back and promised she would have her copies.

The next day, I went to her new home, and after I had been appropriately pampered with tea and snacks by her new in-laws, she handed over a bundle of letters. I left with the originals. The matter of copies was forgotten.

Finally, I had physical evidence of the mystery woman. I was tingling with anticipation as I headed back to my hotel. I couldn't wait to meet her.

But I also dreaded verifying that the love affair, hinted at by my uncle, was actually real.

Part Two

SEVEN

A Passage to America, January–April 1923

Raj remembered the day his passage to America began.

They were all there to see him off. All nine children as well as their mother—sad but determined not to show it—had come to the Quetta railway station. Friends of theirs had also come to wish him well in the new land. He remembered the station's façade, painted in panels of ochre, and framed in white. His older brother was to accompany him as far as Karachi. The two of them were loaded into a compartment and everyone stood around, joking, laughing, crying, while waiting for the train to leave.

His brown suitcase, bought for him by a close friend, contained two suits—one for winter and one, a lighter summer suit, an overcoat heavy enough to withstand the cold of Quetta, and a dozen shirts, including four made of silk. As the train left the platform in a cloud of smoke and steam, he stood at the door of the compartment looking back as his mother's waving figure receded into a speck. He and his brother were on the Bolan Mail, which ran through the foothills of the Himalayas, down into the plains, to the port city of Karachi, where he would embark on his journey to San Francisco.

Karachi, where they arrived days later, was the first large city he had seen. Quetta was much smaller, and most of the buildings there were only one storey. In Karachi, he noticed, the buildings were three, even four storeys, and the roads were wide and paved. There were cars on the streets. There were more people, just in the port area alone, than he had ever seen in all of Quetta. Even Lahore, where he often visited to see his relatives, was smaller by comparison.

Already, he missed the crisp, clean air of Quetta. In coastal Karachi, he was uncomfortable in the humid heat.

But he liked the open skies and spaces. He and his older brother had been cramped in the train for the past few days and, here, despite the heavy, steamy air, he felt his lungs open up as he breathed deeply.

At the port, he saw long, narrow buildings fronting the wide river as it emptied into the sea. The buildings were at least 400 feet tall as they stretched back inland. These must be godowns or warehouses, he surmised. He could see a flurry of activity as dockworkers moved supplies into and out of the buildings. Customs officials, in white uniforms, busied themselves with files and stamps.

Intriguing as this activity was, his eyes were lured by the ocean, further out. The Arabian Sea, at the northern edge of the Indian Ocean, was grey-blue, and he felt his heart waver momentarily. These waters and those of the Pacific would be his home for the next few months. He did not look forward to it.

He saw several ocean liners moored at the port. His ship was to go from Karachi to Bombay; to Penang and to Singapore; and on to Hong Kong where they would stop for three to four days and where he would secure his passage to San Francisco. Then it would be on to Yokohama on another ship; and, finally, the last leg to San Francisco via Honolulu. He would arrive in San Francisco around the third week of April 1923, after an almost three-month journey.

His brother dug him in the ribs, pointed to his ship, and said, 'Your ship seems so small compared to the ones going to Europe.'

'I'm in third class. I'm probably going to sleep on deck, but I'll be comfortable.'

'I know you will. You're happy wherever you are.'

Raj knew his brother was trying to keep things light. The journey, over the *kala pani,* the black waters, as Hindus called the seas, was considered inauspicious. It signified a loss of caste status because one was no longer tied to the land of the Ganges whose waters provided regenerative powers. It broke the cycle of reincarnation. He had dismissed this thought immediately when someone in Quetta had brought it up. He was a Sikh and did not subscribe to the caste system, and his staunch belief was that his destiny was in his hands. Hard work created opportunity and luck, and he was not afraid of hard work. In fact, he relished it.

He smiled at his brother and said, 'Waheguru takes care of me. Why should I worry?'

'I wish you wouldn't bring up God at every turn. Remember, America is a Christian nation; don't get into arguments about religion. Keep your Waheguru to yourself.'

As they walked towards the ramp of the ship, Raj said, 'It should take two days to reach Bombay. I'll send you a telegram from there. It will probably reach Quetta before you get back, but I want Mother to know that I am safe. I'll send you another from Hong Kong, then from Yokohama and, finally, one when I reach San Francisco.'

He saw his brother tearing up and clutched him to his chest. The people left behind were always the more sorrowful, he thought.

'Don't worry. I'll be all right, and I'll come back to all of you and especially to help you to care for the family.'

With that and a final embrace, Raj hefted his suitcase and trudged up the ramp to the top deck. A steward checked his ticket and directed him and the other third-class passengers to the deck below.

'When I boarded the ship, everything was in sixes and sevens. Ropes, planks, wooden boxes, rubbish baskets, were all lying topsy-turvy. We took our luggage downstairs into the passenger's deck. It is an oval room with another room for the engine in the centre below the passenger deck. You can sit anywhere except in the I and II class portion.'

He took off his suit jacket and hung it on one of the pegs. Stowing his suitcase, he went out on the deck, rolling up his sleeves. On the pier, he could see his brother still standing there. He waved, and his brother waved back.

'At 9 P.M. the ship moved out into the middle of the river and stayed there all the night.'

He slept on the top deck.

'On the deck, there are four square openings, about 20'x15'. These opening go right to the bottom of the ship, and when the cargo is stowed away in the hold, these openings are covered over with planks. These planks make a floor a little higher than the deck. They are therefore more advantageous places for sleeping than the surrounding deck. We third-class passengers took a quarter portion of this floor. The first night this place was not covered over with a tarpaulin, and we had to sleep in the open. We could go down to the passenger deck, but that place was warmer.

At about 11 A.M. the next day the ship again began to sail. In the meantime, the deck had been washed, the rubbish was thrown down, the planks adjusted over the openings and everything was in its proper place. The deck was covered over with a tarpaulin. We sat in the shade on the deck. The sea breeze is very pleasant and invigorating. It is just a little lower than body temperature. In the evening there were high winds, and the sailors told us that there would be a storm. The tarpaulin was taken down, and the deck again was uncovered.'

The sun shone fiercely on the deck. He stood looking at the sea as it rushed past below.

~

At Bombay, he got off the ship. They were going to be there for two days, and he wanted to use the time available to walk around the city and see some of the sites. He also remembered he had promised to send a telegram to his mother.

After Bombay, the days at sea began to take on a rhythm. When he had washed up and eaten breakfast, he would walk round and round the top deck for two to three hours. The fresh breeze energized him. In a secluded corner of the deck, he did push-ups and squats. Most of the time, he remained on the deck, since the tiny cabin made him claustrophobic. If he was not exercising, he would engage in discourses with fellow passengers. Lunch and dinner were anti-climactic: the food was plentiful but had no taste. The only redeeming feature was that there was milk to drink.

From the deck, whether he was walking or exercising, or just leaning on the rail, he saw the landscape of western, and then southern, India slipping past. Trees that he was not used to seeing were in abundance here: palm trees with waving fronds clustered all along the shore. White, sandy beaches rushed past. He had never been on a beach and wondered what the ocean's water would feel like. As the land receded inland, it rose perceptibly from the sea level of the beaches to a higher plateau. Just-remembered geography lessons reminded him he was going past the Western Ghats, the ramparts rising to become the Deccan Plateau that dominated the topography of southern India. Verdant forests covered the slopes and heights of the plateau. He was not used to so much greenery. Quetta's landscape was brown, dusty, and rocky. Here the land was lush, green, and covered with trees. He was also not used to the humidity. His shirt stuck to his back. But if there was a breeze, he was refreshed. Someone on deck told him that in a month or so, the summer monsoons would lash the region and the temperature would dip a little, but the humidity would remain all year long.

Almost a week after they left Karachi, the ship reached the first major stop of the journey, Penang, where he mailed a letter back home. '*All the passengers were examined by the doctor, and the ship stayed there for three hours. There were nearly 70 Chinese passengers who came on board.*'

On the way to Singapore, he wrote, '*The sea was dark blue on the way to Penang, but here it was greenish blue. At night, the sea was alight with myriad fluorescent fishes. It looked like the sky with stars. Along the ship, there was a cloud of light like the milky way. After an hour we will reach Singapore.*'

A few days later, on 22 April, the ship reached Hong Kong, its destination. He would have to find another ship to take him to San Francisco and secure his passage on it.

~

He had heard there were many Sikhs in Hong Kong employed by the British in their police and military forces. He found it surprising that the British would use the colonized of one country to help police another colony. But, he surmised, it fit in their divide and rule concept. He hoped there was a gurdwara in Hong Kong where he could stay.

As he descended the ramp onto Hong Kong's pier, he saw the same style of warehouses he had seen in Karachi. Beyond them was a busy street. He was pleasantly surprised to see a Sikh policeman on a small circular platform in the centre of the intersection. Like the structures he had seen in Quetta, the platform had three concrete columns supporting a domed roof. It was like a large umbrella, and it provided much-needed shade.

It seems, he thought, the British had copied it in other colonies.

His mother's advice came to him: if you are in a strange place and need help, ask the first Sikh for assistance; he will help you as a fellow Sikh. He had questioned his mother on this: Why would they help me?

'You see, we are a small community, and we try to help each other as much as we can. Help is never refused to another Sikh. That's why you see lots of beggars on the streets in India but never a Sikh beggar. Never.'

He was about to test the helping part of that statement.

He made his way to the edge of the road, placed his suitcase on the ground, and stood staring at the policeman, hoping he would notice him. Soon, the policeman, perhaps feeling his stare, acknowledged his presence and motioned for him to wait where he was.

After about fifteen minutes, during which time he remained motionless on the curb against the flow of traffic, he saw another policeman, also a Sikh, come to relieve the first policeman.

The first policeman came over to him and greeted him in the traditional manner. 'Sat Sri Akal,' he said. 'Did you just get off that boat? My name is Manmohan Singh. What's yours?'

He was relieved to see that the policeman was friendly and looked helpful. He introduced himself and said, 'Yes, I came on that boat from Karachi. We'll be here for a few days, and I must buy a ticket to America. I have the name of a friend of our family. He lives in Kowloon. His name is Jamadar Puran Singh, head clerk of the 102 Grenadiers. Can you direct me to this address?'

'The 102 Grenadiers? Yes, they've been stationed here since the end of the First World War.'

Much to his delight, the policeman said that his shift was over, and he could take him to meet Puran Singh. He protested that it wasn't necessary for the policeman to go out of his way.

The policeman brushed aside his objections, 'It's a long way, and you'll have to take a tram and a bus. So, let me take you there.' With that, the policeman picked up the suitcase and led the way.

On the journey, the policeman told him that the Sikh policemen and military, recruited from the Punjab by the British to establish law and order in Hong Kong, had built three gurdwaras in Hong Kong. He told him they had plenty of room for students like him. 'If Puran Singh can't house you, you can stay at one of them.'

The nearest gurdwara, he told him, was in the Wan Chai district on Queen Street.

He was tired and hungry. He wanted some food and a real bed that was not rolling with the waves. Hong Kong was even more crowded than Karachi, and on a much larger scale, but he did not find it forbidding. Most of the buildings were three-storeyed, the streets were paved, and there was an electric tram.

An hour later, they reached the offices of the 102 Grenadiers. Jamadar Puran Singh was delighted to see him. 'Your older brother is one of my best friends, and he helped me a lot in securing this job.'

While it was clear that the soldier was ready to help, he lived in army quarters, so Raj would have to stay in the gurdwara. 'Let me sign off, and I'll take you there,' Jamadar Puran Singh said.

The three of them set off, the policeman indicating that this would give him an opportunity to have langar at the Queen Street gurdwara. The gurdwara was a deep, two-storeyed building, and seemed to have been a private residence at one time. There was a wide veranda on both floors fronting the street. He was thankful for this and other gurdwaras where one could ask for food and lodging. Those, he knew, would be provided free, for as long as he wanted. He would have to perform some community service for the congregants, he knew. But he felt that would enrich him.

The policeman introduced him to the person who took care of the gurdwara. The gurdwara secretary took him to what would be his room for the next few days. It was on the second floor, towards the back of the building. It had a comfortable bed, a window that looked out over the back garden and an easy chair. The window was open, and Hong Kong's humid, balmy breeze wafted in, lifting the curtains. Down the hall was the communal bathroom, which was spotlessly clean.

He had a quick shower, changed his clothes, re-tied his turban, and went down to the lunch hall. The policeman and the soldier were seated on the floor. They had finished langar and were drinking tea laced with cardamom. As soon as he sat down on the floor beside them, someone brought him a plate with black daal and phulkas. The people of the community—women and men—would have cooked this meal as they did every day. He noticed about twenty others having lunch. Some were Chinese. Some congregants were helping in serving the food, and they came around every few minutes with small buckets of the daal and baskets of phulkas to replenish plates.

After lunch was over, both his benefactors said their goodbyes. The policeman invited him and Jamadar Puran Singh to his house for dinner the next day. Raj offered profuse thanks, but the policeman waved him off.

'Pay this back by helping another Sikh who needs help, will you? That's thanks enough for me.'

When they had left, the gurdwara secretary sat down beside him.

'There are about 2,000 Sikhs in Hong Kong and a tenth of them, as well as non-Sikhs, eat at the gurdwara every day,' he told him. The secretary asked him how long he would be staying. He said the ship would leave in four days. The secretary told him he could stay as long as he needed and that, as he was a student and new to Hong Kong, he did not have to worry about doing anything in the gurdwara.

'Just make your bed and keep your room and the bathroom clean after you use it. Go out and explore Hong Kong.' With that, he took him to his office and gave him a map. He also asked if he needed any money.

'No,' he told the secretary. 'I have some.'

But the secretary pressed a few notes into his hand and said, 'Here's some local currency for you to use.'

He went that afternoon to the offices of the shipping company and bought a ticket to San Francisco for 750 rupees, roughly $250.

That night, seated on his bed in the gurdwara, he hastily scribbled a stilted note home to his brother.

'Puran Singh remembers you much and thinks of you as one of his great friends.

My passage to San Francisco has been arranged on S.S. Taiyo Maru. *I have bought the ticket for Rupees 750/-. The ship sails on the 24th instant.*

I will send you a parcel with pairs of slippers, and I will also put this letter in it.

*The weather here is very pleasant. It rains nearly once a day. I can wear my warm suit here.'**

The next day, he explored Hong Kong on foot. He went up the Peak Tramway to Victoria Peak to get a grand vista of the island as well as some parts of the Mainland. He walked back to Victoria Harbour and took the Star Ferry across the harbour to Kowloon. There, as he walked the streets with its lively markets, he noticed many statues of the Buddha in shops and marvelled at how that religion had taken root in China. He ate grilled meats at one of the roadside food stands. It was excellent, spicy, and charred. It reminded him somewhat of the kebabs in Quetta's food stands where he was discouraged from eating by his mother.

That night he went to the policeman's house and met his family. Over dinner, the policeman's family and especially his son, Deep, peppered him with questions about America. 'I don't know much about it,' he admitted. 'I haven't been there, but I'll send you postcards if you like.'

The next day he went to the grandly built Kowloon-Canton railway terminus building, which was bustling

---

* The italicized portions are excerpts from letters my father wrote home to his elder brother who saved them. They are now in my possession.

inside. Streams of mainland Chinese were coming into Hong Kong with their bundles of belongings. They would settle here or, like him, find passage to America to start new lives. He looked up at the clock tower attached to the terminus building. It must be at least 140 feet high, he thought. He went inside and climbed the wooden stairs to the top of the tower. From there he had another vista of Hong Kong, looking out over the harbour to Kowloon. Docked in the harbour was the *Taiyo Maru* which he would be boarding soon. He saw workers cleaning the ship's decks and others bringing on provisions for the sailing to Yokohama.

When he boarded the ship, the policeman and his family were there to see him off. His wife had brought a box full of chapattis, vegetables and meat for the journey. It was supposed to last a couple of days, but he shared it with his new friends on board, and it was all gone that evening.

One of his new friends who especially liked the home-cooked Indian food was Hana Monai, '*a pretty Japanese teacher who taught English at Kyoto Imperial University*'. He must have made an impression on her because, when they docked in Kyoto on 6 May, she took him to her lodgings at Professor Nishida's.

Kitaro Nishida was a prominent philosopher in Japan and had started the Kyoto School of philosophy. For a few days, he stayed there and was enchanted by the wooden houses, the custom of '*wearing straw shoes inside the house… Every house has a little garden, which is laid out like nature. They place big irregular pieces of stones here and there and leave circuitous paths in between. The trees are of a wild nature. The*

Japanese are famous for their trees. They grow a bonsai tree in small pots, and you can find trees 50 to 80 years old simply one foot high.'

While he was happy with Hana's company, what pleased him more were the discussions he had with Professor Nishida, and he was pleasantly surprised at the professor's curiosity about Sikh religious philosophy. He was delighted at his host's openness.

'*One thing that I have learned about living in foreign nations is not to be shy and to say whatever is at the tip of your tongue.*'

With Hana as a travelling guide, he saw '*Nagasaki, Osaka, Kyoto and Tokyo. Throughout my stay, we experienced mild weather.*'

On 11 May, the *Taiyo Maru* sailed for Honolulu and would arrive there eleven days later. A tearful Hana had come to the port to see him off. From Honolulu, San Francisco was a five-day voyage.

On 26 May 1923, his ship docked at the outside port in San Francisco at 8 am. The passengers were inspected by a quarantine officer who came on board to conduct examinations. After being cleared by him, they could proceed to the wharf where, in the shelter of a huge building, an immigration officer checked his papers and logged him into the List or Manifest of Alien Passengers for the United States. His travel document was a British Indian passport. He gave them his details and his older brother's name as his nearest relative from his country of origin. His nationality was listed as British subject and his race as East Indian.

'Here there is a very good but expensive luggage transfer

system. The agents of the company come to the ship and give their labels. We attach the labels to our luggage and get a receipt for them and give them our address on the label. After this, we have nothing to do with our luggage. The company brings it safely to your address.'

Having thus freed himself of his luggage, he went '*by ferry to Berkeley and paid eighteen cents for my fare*'. There he went to 2026 Centre Street, to the Hindustan Club for Indian students. That evening some Sikh students took him to the Khalsa Club.

The next day he went back to Berkeley to finalize his admission at the University. He gave his details to the admissions officer and gave her his letter notifying him of his acceptance.

Everything, the admissions officer said, was in order and he could begin his classes in August. However, he soon learnt that he could not take summer classes and, as his meagre money could only last so long, he looked for an alternative college. A friend told him about the University of Illinois, and he contacted them. He felt lucky that he was considered for and finally admitted to the University of Illinois, Urbana-Champaign campus.

He had also been told by his friends that there was a gurdwara in Stockton, some eighty miles from San Francisco. It had been built by immigrant Sikhs in 1912 and was the first gurdwara in America.

He went to the Stockton gurdwara, arriving at the end of May 1923. He had been planning to take a bus, but his friends insisted on driving him. They arrived just in time for langar, and his friends decided they wanted some of the tasty langar food.

The gurdwara in Stockton was a two-storey building, a little smaller than the one in Hong Kong, but similar in structure. It had once been a farmhouse. He was shown to a small room on the second floor. He left his small suitcase in the room and went down to join his friends and the other congregants for langar.

At the end of the langar, he was introduced to the small congregation. Most, he found out, were farmers in the nearby San Joaquin Valley, centred around San Jose. However, one of the founders of the gurdwara, Bhagwan Singh, had over 500 acres near Holt, a small town that they had passed on the way to Stockton.

They were seated together in the langar hall, and Bhagwan Singh was telling him his story in Punjabi and badly-accented English.

'When the first Sikhs migrated to California in the early 1900s they, like me, had come from farming backgrounds in the Punjab. My family had a large farm near Hoshiarpur in the Punjab. We saw that the climate and the soil in California was very similar to the conditions in the Punjab.'

'Yes,' Raj interrupted, 'it reminds me of land around Baluchistan and the Lyallpur Hills.'

Bhagwan Singh nodded. 'As I was saying, we had no skills other than farming. I have no education to speak of: I dropped out of school after the 8th grade. But, like the others, I wanted to cultivate and farm the land. However, there was a California state law that barred us from owning land. The law had been passed to exclude the Japanese and Chinese immigrants from owning land, but it netted the Indians too.'

Raj thought that the law was racist in its intent and said so to the farmer.

'I guess keeping what you have for those like you is common all over the world. In any case, the Sikhs leased the land from the owners and started fruit, cotton, and almond orchards in the San Joaquin Valley. Most were centred around Yuba City. I chose to go to Holt because it was close to the Middle River and the canal system. At first, I too leased land from a white American. On my leased land, I started growing cotton, and I had some peach orchards. Then I noticed there were Mexican women, who had fled Mexico's Civil War, and who worked as labourers on the farms. I found out that they could own land. But they did not have money. Here we had a perfect coincidence—we wanted to own the lands, the Mexican women wanted to pull themselves up. I noticed a particularly beautiful Mexican girl, Carmen Alvarez, who reminded me of a Sikh girl I had liked in my hometown in India. I did not speak Spanish, and she did not speak English, or Punjabi for that matter.'

Here Bhagwan Singh gave a small chuckle.

'So how did you communicate?'

'I can't say that love helped us. We spoke in a mix of the little Spanish that I could muster and the bit of English she knew. We managed. Eventually, we got married. She kept her maiden name, so she could register the land in her name. Now the farm is in her name, but we work it together.'

Raj took the opportunity to ask, 'And you're happy?'

'Look, it's not too different from our arranged marriages, is it? Only we chose each other.'

'How long have you been married now?'

'About fifteen years. And ours isn't the only marriage like this. I know of many. Someone told me that there are about 400 Sikh men married to Mexican women.'

'Are these other marriages successful? I mean, these were marriages of convenience, weren't they?'

'Yes, they were. But the couples thrived. We learned that our cultural habits and food were not that different from each other. We Sikh men taught our Mexican wives to make phulkas and daal. These are not far from their tortillas and beans. We taught them to incorporate Indian spices and techniques into Mexican food. They, too, use cumin, coriander and cilantro. We have the most delicious meals on these farms—carnitas with saag, chicken curry enchiladas, keema empanadas, you name it. Carmen and I have two children, and we gave them Americanized names: Camille and David. Our children can speak Punjabi and Spanish.'

Raj could see that the farmer was very proud of his accomplishments and complimented him fervently on this.

Then Bhagwan Singh turned to him and said, 'I have an idea. Why don't you come out to the farm with me? If you're not doing anything, you can work for me. I'll pay you 40 cents an hour. That's $4.40 a day if you work 11 hours, like the rest. We provide meals, and you'll have to sleep in the camp we have for workers. You'll be charged 70 cents daily for food and lodging, but you can eat all the fruit you want, and I'll make sure that you're well fed. There are some other Sikh students there as well, so you'll have their company.'

His mind was in a whirl. He did have a few weeks before his classes started in Illinois. He also needed the money. It sounded like a godsend. 'Why not,' he found himself saying. 'I'd be happy to work for you. I know nothing of farming, but I learn quickly. I must tell you, also, that in a couple of months' time I will have to leave and go to the university to study engineering.'

'Oh, that's all right,' Bhagwan Singh said. 'It's harvest time for the peaches now. I can use your help. Besides, you're better educated than the other people there, and you can give me some advice on running the farm. Let's go.'

He collected his belongings and said his thank yous and goodbyes to the gurdwara secretary. Then they got into Bhagwan Singh's pickup truck, a Chevrolet Roadster, and made their way through farmlands to his farm. On the drive, Raj told Bhagwan Singh about his background and they got into a discussion on Sikhism, and on how it was difficult for Bhagwan Singh to practice it.

The farm, as Bhagwan Singh had promised, was beautiful. He passed a dozen or so workers, mostly men but some women too, in the fields.

'Are those borewells, I see?'

'Yes, they are. I can irrigate over 100 acres with one of these. Later, if you want, you can tend to the wells. It's a longer day, but the work is very easy: all you have to do is to re-direct the flow to different water channels every few hours.'

He was shown to the worker's camp, and the foreman showed him to his hut and found an empty cot for him where he deposited his suitcase. Within an hour of his arrival, he was hard at work.

After the cramped confines of the ship, he was happy to be outside, doing physical work. '*Now I will tell you what we have to do here. All the Sikh students work in the fields. We have to do every kind of field work: hoeing, plowing, picking the cotton, or plucking the fruits. The work is very hard and strenuous, but after some time one gets used to it. We get up early in the morning at five, and then after taking some tea and bread, we go to work at six. We reach the farm at six-thirty, and we hoe the field up to twelve. The field is cultivated with cotton and vine, and we have to take out the weeds and grass. We rest from twelve to one and then work up to five-fifteen and reach our camp at six. In this way, we work eleven hours.*'

After the first hour that first day, his body got used to the motions and his mind was free to think and dream. His back became accustomed to the bending he had to do to clear the weeds and lift the boxes of peaches onto truck beds. He had his fill of fresh fruit, which he loved. He never forgot how a freshly picked peach tasted: the flavours, the juiciness, the colours. He became a connoisseur of peaches and could tell just by looking whether one was ripe or not, whether it was going to be sweet.

During the short lunch break, Mrs Alvarez and some of the Mexican women would bring food to the fields, and they would eat in the shade of the orchard trees. They had tortillas or phulkas, depending on Mrs Alvarez's mood, with spicy beef curry or pork carnitas. There was lemonade and fresh well-water, and plenty of creamy, whole milk. It did not matter whether it was sunny, cloudy, or rainy. He worked through them all and became one with the land and the farm.

One evening, after he had washed up, Bhagwan Singh invited him for dinner to the house. He joined the farmer's family, Mrs Alvarez and their two children. After dinner, he and the farmer sat on the porch and talked late into the night, drinking strong milky tea laced with ginger—just the way it was drunk in India.

'Tell me, you're an educated man. You have an undergraduate degree from Quetta in mathematics, you said. Can you help me with my books? I need to set up a system so I can track my income and expenditures. Now, I just keep the receipts, and all that information is in my head. If I have money in the bank account, I know I'm ahead. But by how much, I don't know.'

'I'd be happy to help you. But I must warn you, I'm no accountant. I can set up a ledger for you, though.'

Bhagwan Singh then said, 'How about my irrigation system? Or marketing my peaches? You have suggestions?'

Raj wasn't a farmer, but he was astute. He had seen where improvements could be made to the wells and the water flow. He delved into those with enthusiasm.

'We have the makings of a good partnership,' Bhagwan Singh said. 'Why don't you buy the neighbouring parcel of land? I'll help you finance it. Together we'll be the most productive cooperative.'

'I would love to stay here. I like this work. But I promised myself and, most importantly, my mother that I would become an engineer, gain some work experience, and then return to Quetta. I keep my promises.'

'OK, OK, my God, has anyone told you that you're quite focused and passionate about your aims? Nothing will ever deter you, will it? But tell me, can you teach my family something about Sikhism. Not the kind of details you were telling me earlier on our ride back to the farm. That made even my head hurt. So much philosophy! But just the basics. I don't know much of it myself because I was never taught these things. All of us in the family would benefit from your knowledge.'

He laughed at this and said, 'Certainly, it'll be my pleasure. I can come around after work from time to time and tell you what you want to know. Also, if Camille and David have any difficulties with math I can teach them.'

'That's great. Whenever they come to me or go to their mother for any help on any subject, we're lost. I want them to be educated like you when they grow up. Farming is good, but education is more important.'

Soon, he was a constant in their household. Those nights when he went to their house, he would sleep in the spare bedroom of the main house. He would be up at dawn and eat warm tortillas doused in fried eggs covered in hot ranchero sauce, drink strong coffee and then head out to the fields. Sometimes, with the farmer's permission, he would go to the barn and drink milk from the cow's udders, as had been his custom in Quetta. Mrs Alvarez and little Camille thought this was disgusting, as did many of the other Mexican hands.

At the end of two months, he had to leave to get to Illinois to join his university course. The farmer wanted him to stay. His family wanted him to stay. Mrs Alvarez said 'You know Maria in our packing department has taken a liking to you. Why don't you stay and marry her? You can buy land together.'

Bhagwan Singh reiterated his offer to loan him money

to buy the adjoining farm. But he told them that his mind was set on becoming an engineer.

Bhagwan Singh patted him on the back and said, 'I will not stand in the way of your destiny and your stubbornness. But promise me you'll come back here if you have breaks and work alongside me. There will always be a job for you. And here is your money.' Raj could see it was more than what he was owed and began to protest.

'I'm paying you for all the education you have given my family and me. My wells are the best. My farm equipment runs better than it used to. The children's test scores have improved. We've all learned a little about Sikhism. I'm not paying you enough. But, when you have a lot of money, as I know you will, you can contribute it back to a gurdwara. Will you do that for me?'

He readily agreed and, with a final wave to the family and workers, he set off.

He had arrived in America and was ready for the next task at hand: an engineering degree.

EIGHT

13 April 1927

It had been four years since Raj arrived in America. He was an engineer now, with a job at Bucyrus Erie, in Milwaukee, Wisconsin, where he was getting the work experience he needed. Soon, he would be headed home to Quetta.

On this day though, he was looking forward to meeting friends at the Chicago gurdwara to take part in the Sikh New Year celebration.

Wednesdays were usually slow at Bucyrus Erie, and his boss, Mr Fykes, had readily agreed when Raj asked for the day off.

In his Punjab, Baisakhi was a day for much celebration, coinciding with the spring harvest, when the winter crops were reaped. There would be many fairs in different parts of Quetta and the surrounding villages. Selling their crops of wheat, barley, mustard, sesame and green peas, the farmers would be flush with cash and in a festive mood as they made their way among the many food stalls and, later, took part in the impromptu bhangra and gidda dancing that went on late into the evening. He wondered what the festivities in Chicago would be like. Not much dancing, he figured, but at least he would be with friends.

All of March had been unseasonably warm in Milwaukee, and the warm weather had continued into April. But on 13 April, when the sun's pleasant heat would have reminded Raj of Quetta, it started raining. The sky opened up, and it poured.

The North Shore line ran a two-hour interurban service from Milwaukee to Chicago. At the new terminal building, wet with rain, Raj waited for the Chicago Limited, train number 414, scheduled to leave Milwaukee at 11 a.m. It would arrive in Chicago at 1:05 p.m. Later, he would catch the 6 p.m. train back.

For Raj, the best part of the train was the parlour-buffet car, where green-cushioned wicker chairs could be arranged next to portable tables to eat snacks and meals. On other trips, he had gone into the buffet car to buy a sandwich, and he knew the meagre menu by heart. Thinking of the parlour car, he realized he was hungry, but decided to wait until Racine to get himself something. He knew the price of a coffee was 25 cents and that a '*flaky-crust home-made pie*' was 30 cents. They always had his favourite pie made of apples with cinnamon mixed in. The 55 cents would meet the minimum charge per person, and this snack would also sustain him until Chicago and the langar at the gurdwara. He knew he had about 65 cents change, which he carried in a cleverly designed small change pocket that the Quetta tailor had made, stitched into the front waistband of his trousers.

He was always aware, in fact, of the exact amount of money he had on him and in the bank. His resources were slim, and he tried to save every penny he could to send back home.

He was dressed in the warmer suit that had been tailored for him in Quetta. While it was deemed fashionable there—cut in an English style, like those of the British officers he saw in the barracks area in Quetta—it was out of place in Milwaukee. The charcoal-gray herringbone pattern accentuated the lapels that were too narrow for the styles of the day. The jacket was also cut a bit too short. The suit was threadbare and hung loosely on his frame. He had lost weight during the four years in America; the hours of hard physical work, first on the farm and now at the foundry, had burnt off a lot of calories. His meals, too, were meagre, not at all like the ones in Quetta, where he and all eight of his siblings sat around a large table eating the tasty dishes prepared by their mother. His meals in the States were sandwiches for lunch, and soup and a hot plate special at the local diner for dinner.

He hoped the worn-down, ill-fitting suit might not attract much attention. But he figured his turban—of a light, blue-grey colour—and his full, black bushy beard probably would. He realized his turban was getting a bit tired-looking after all the years of wear and tear. It was also soggy with rain, as were his cheap shoes.

He knew he cut a strange figure but perhaps one that might be considered exotic. Rudolph Valentino's *The Sheik* had been quite the rage a few years earlier, and while Raj did not like being mistaken for an Arab, at least it was a positive image and a head-turner for women.

He got onto the train with a handful of other passengers and chose the first car near the engine because it would be closer to the exit in Chicago. The train smelled damp and stuffy with the odour of wool, wet from rain. He settled into a seat that faced forward: Raj hated travelling backwards because it made him nauseous, and he couldn't see where he was headed. He liked to see the future coming at him and not flying past.

He closed his eyes and waited for one of his favourite moments: when the porter yelled 'All Aboard' and the large electric motors whined into gear, beginning at a low pitch, and then going higher and higher as the train gained speed. A horn from the train sounded a warning—here in Milwaukee, the train ran on city streets, on tracks of steel, and sleepers specially built of concrete.

As the train made its way out of the depot, its sounds changed as it went over the long viaduct that crossed both channels of the Menomonee River. Racine and coffee were about a half hour away. From his coat pocket, Raj dug out a notebook and a small gutka—the booklet containing most of the important prayers and sections of the Guru Granth Sahib. The notebook, dog-eared and well-used, was where he made notes on his readings.

The train went over the Root River Bridge before arriving at the Racine station, a long, low building with a pitched roof that extended over the platform to give protection from inclement weather.

Raj looked out and saw there were two passengers waiting for the train. One was an elderly woman, her stout figure bundled up in indistinguishable black and grey clothing. But the other caught his eye.

As his car passed, she looked up and smiled at him and, instantly, he felt the force of the smile. He leaned forward and looked back down the platform at her. She was wearing a black-and-white-checked wool coat that came just below her knees. It had a fur collar of a deep grey that framed her oval face. On her hands were small black gloves, on her head, a small cloche hat with a saucy plumed feather. The porter was talking to her, and she gestured towards her bag. He took it to the baggage car and, as she was about to step onto the train, she looked directly at Raj. He had a glimpse of a shapely calf and a fine ankle; on her feet were low-heeled grey suede shoes. He shrank from the window and sank into his chair. His ears were burning, and he felt he was blushing. Strange that the one look so disconcerted him.

Flustered, he began to look at the gutka, but the words were blurred. The train had resumed its rhythm, except now it was flying south on a straight track, speeding by Lake Michigan on his left.

Time for a snack, he thought, having shaken off the image of the woman.

He got up and, instinctively, his hands went up to make sure his turban was sitting well on his head. Then, he started walking towards the parlour car. As he came into the connecting corridor, he saw the men's toilet and ducked in. Standing in front of the mirror, he brushed his jacket, straightened, and centred his tie. He brushed back his beard, twirled his moustache ends. Why, he thought, was he doing all this?

The parlour car looked empty. But as Raj stepped in, he immediately saw her sitting at a table to his right, her legs crossed; her coat was draped over an empty chair. She had, he saw now, a finely sculpted face. Her hair was shoulder length, held back by a barrette under the cloche. Her dress was a cream-coloured sheath, pleated below the waist. Along the edge of the skirt and the cropped sleeves was a band of navy trim. She was remarkably beautiful, he thought, very self-possessed, assured in her elegance and beauty.

Unaware of his scrutiny, she was intent on a game of solitaire. Her long, elegant fingers caressed the cards. Though he was not a card player, he did play solitaire at times. He wasn't good at it, but he'd developed some shortcuts.

As he shut the door behind him, she turned and looked up at him. Her eyes were sparkling. The sides of her mouth were turning up in a smile and she said 'good morning' in an even and inviting voice.

'Good morning,' he managed and hurried along to the bar. The counterman, dressed in a white jacket, a white shirt with a green bowtie, and green trousers, took his order. He paid for his food and turned to find an empty table. Then he saw that she was pointing to the chair next to her.

'Why don't you come and join me?' she said. He walked over to her table, careful not to spill any coffee. 'No point for the two of us to sit alone, is there? I saw you looking out the window, and thought to myself: What an interesting-looking man. I was hoping I would see you again and, well, here you are!'

She had a disarming manner—her eyes were clear and blue, and she looked at him with a direct, inquisitive gaze. The way she had spoken to him, directly and without hesitation, made it clear she was not a demure woman.

Now she was smiling, and there was no awkwardness in her behaviour. He had met few women like her, though he was reminded of a distant relative in India—a strong woman who conducted herself as everyone's equal, her elder male relatives included. Yes, he thought, as he sat down, the woman in front of him was just like Rukman: an independent, confident woman, sure of her own attractiveness and allure. He felt desire stir within him. He may have been hesitant but he, too, was a self-confident person.

He looked down at the table where she had spread out her solitaire game. 'I can show you how to finish that game mathematically and in a short time,' he said.

'Thank you, please do,' she said, laughing.

'I like that line,' she continued, 'no one has used that on me before. I was getting a bit bored sitting by myself with this game. I can play it anywhere. May I ask you a question?'

He sensed what it would be. 'Of course,' he said, 'ask me anything you want.'

'That headpiece you have on: It's really very beautiful. It must take you a long time to tie it. Do you tie it every day?'

And then, impishly, she leaned forward and said, with a flirty laugh in her voice, 'Do you wear it in bed?'

He was used to these questions—not the last one though, which was quite unexpected. Looking across at her now, he saw that, as she leaned forward, her V-neck had suddenly become deeper and fuller.

'No, I don't wear it to bed. Yes, I tie it every day. Do you want to know how long it is?' he added, turning a little crimson at the unintended double entendre.

'Yes, tell me all about it! Tell me all about you!' she said.

'Well,' he said, regaining some of his composure, 'it's five yards long and a yard and a quarter wide. I have turbans in many colours in India but here, in America, I only have about a half dozen. In India, where I come from, I have some printed with polka dots or with stripes. But I prefer plainer colours: blue-grey like this one, or beige. What else can I tell you? But, first, may I offer you something to drink: a cup of coffee, perhaps?'

'Sure, that would be nice. But don't get up. I'll get Steve to bring me one. He knows me. In fact, all the porters on this train know me. I go to Chicago every week. I teach piano there.'

With that, she looked at the counterman who seemed to have been waiting for her signal.

He hurried over. 'The usual, Mrs Lutes?' he asked.

'Yes, Steve, good morning. How are you today?' she said. And she ordered a cup of black coffee with no cream and no sugar.

When the counterman left, she said to him, apologetically: 'I would have introduced you, but I don't know your name.' As she said this, she reached forward and touched his hand. It burnt under her cool fingers.

He told her his name.

'That's very masculine sounding. But what am I saying? Sorry, I don't mean to be rude!' and she leaned forward again and touched his hand.

Steve returned with her coffee. He also brought a couple of shortbread biscuits. 'I thought you'd like this, Mrs Lutes, seeing as it's early and you may have had nothing to eat for breakfast. It's a long drive to Racine for you to catch this train, isn't it?'

After the counterman left, she said, 'Oh, that Steve, he's nice. They all take good care of me, you know. Listen, I didn't mean to be impolite, but can I shorten your name so it's easier for me to remember? Just in case, you know,' giving him a sidelong, appraising, glance.

This was all going too fast for him. He had never met a woman quite like her. She was interested in him, he sensed, but her forwardness seemed, also, to set off alarms in his head. To regain control, he took a bite of the apple pie and a long sip of his coffee. Both were very reassuring.

He gave a shortened version of his name. 'Raj,' he said, 'you can call me Raj if you want.'

As he spoke, he was inwardly wincing. Growing up, his parents had insisted on calling him and his siblings by their given names. He was always Rajinder Singh to his parents and to his family. There were no nicknames allowed. In fact, not only were they called by their given names but their middle names, Singh for all the males, and Kaur for the females, as required in the Sikh faith, were also attached. And now, here he was, shortening his name for a woman he'd just met. What was going on?

'Raj! Oh, that's so much easier. I'll call you Raj and you can call me Louise, or anything else you want.' And, once more, those eyes glittered with a coquettish look.

'Steve called you Mrs Lutes,' he said, trying to seize the initiative. 'Are you married?'

'Oh, no, that's done with. I'm divorced. Look, no ring!' Once again, she leaned forward and touched his hand. 'You don't have to worry about that!' And now, he was sure that she was flirting.

'Tell me, why are you going to Chicago? Do you know someone there? A special someone?' she continued.

He was sure there was a wink and a nudge in that question. He had begun to enjoy her friendly flirting and decided to drop his serious air.

'No, no one special, but I was hoping I'd meet someone special on this train. Is that you?' he asked. This time he reached forward and touched her hand. He noticed her long fingers. Artistic, he thought to himself.

He noticed also that she did not withdraw her hands.

'Well, Raj! What a thought. A nice thought, isn't it? Oh, we do have a lot to talk about, don't we? I want to know everything about you. But, really, tell me, why are you going to Chicago?' she asked.

'I'm a Sikh,' he said, pointing to his turban. 'Today is our New Year. We call it Baisakhi. I'm going to Chicago to meet some friends and go to the gurdwara, our temple, for a special service. One of my friends will pick me up in his car and we'll drive there. Then he'll drop me back in Chicago in time for the Milwaukee Limited at 6 p.m. I have to work tomorrow.' He knew he was flustered and providing unnecessary details.

Her eyes dimmed. He could see she was disappointed.

'Does that mean we can't spend time together in Chicago? I'm free all day and my piano lessons aren't until tomorrow. Are you sure?'

He realized, at once, that he wanted to be with her.

He was caught in a dilemma. He really wanted to go to the gurdwara. Just listening to the kirtan always grounded him. He was also hankering for some Punjabi food. He couldn't let his friends down. They had all made special efforts to be together. Surely, there must be a way.

Perhaps there was. He could meet her for an early dinner and then sleep over at his friend Bawa's place. Bawa could run him to the station the next morning in time to catch the 7:15 a.m. Badger Limited to Milwaukee. That would get in at 9:22 a.m. and, if he took a cab, he could be at work by 9:45 a.m. He was sure he had enough for the fare. He'd forego a few lunches to make up for the cab fare. He would be late, but he could hopefully be allowed to make up for it by staying late, into the evening shift. Or he could work extra lunch hours the next few days. Mr Fykes liked him and would probably allow it, he thought, but not without a lecture on punctuality and responsibility.

There was, however, another problem. Louise was very beautiful, and there was no doubt she was attracted to him. He was sure, too, that he was interested in her. His mother's admonishments, though, came back to him. She had made it clear she expected him back in India after his degree was finished, and he had acquired some work experience. She would rely on him to help bring up his younger siblings. So, she had said, if there is any entanglement you get into, and she specifically meant an affair of the heart, 'run away from it. Run away and don't look back. Come back to us.'

He looked up at Louise. She was still holding his hands, and her eyes had an insistent look.

'OK, here's what I can do,' he said and proceeded to lay out the possibilities. 'If you like we can have an early dinner and then I can take the 8 p.m. train back to Milwaukee.' He did not want to tell her, for some reason, that he would sleep over at Bawa's.

She clapped her hands in delight.

'Thank you, Raj,' she said. 'I can get to know you better and we can talk over dinner. Yes, an early dinner is just what I had in mind. I stay at the Auditorium Hotel in Chicago. Do you know it? It has a very nice restaurant. I stay at the hotel every week, so they've given me a long-term lease on a little apartment instead of just a bedroom. Let's do that. What time do you think you can come?'

They were just flying past the Nash Motors plant at Kenosha. The air horns were shrieking every few minutes as the train went past the in-plant crosswalks.

Collecting himself, he turned towards her and said, as evenly as he could, 'I can get there around six this evening. My friend is going to drop me off at the Roosevelt Road terminus of the NSL about 5:45 p.m. Where is the Auditorium Hotel?'

'It's at Congress and Michigan. Why don't you ask him to drop you off there? The hotel is about a mile from the terminus.'

'No, it's OK. I'm used to walking. Besides, walking clears my head,' he said. Actually, he thought, I don't want Bawa to know where I'm going because that would bring up tiresome questions and crude jokes.

'Maybe you can come up to my room and have a cup of coffee first. I hope it stops raining. But it doesn't look as though it will. Anyway, you can come up and dry out a bit before dinner, if you're caught in the rain. Would that be OK?'

Her voice, while tentative, was insistent. He could feel that she was a strong-willed woman used to having her way.

'You know,' she continued, 'my room has a nice view of Grant Park and Lake Michigan. It's one of my favourite things to do: watch dusk come down and the lights of Chicago going on in the early evening. Everything seems so peaceful. Down below, in the streets, I know, there's a lot of traffic and people scurrying to get the L. But up in my room, I can sit back in my armchair and relax with a drink before dinner. Do you drink?'

He had been lulled by her voice and the tranquillity she was describing, so that her question startled him a bit.

'No, I don't. My religion forbids it. But I don't mind if you drink. In fact, anything that relaxes you is good, isn't it?'

'I suppose so,' she said. 'What relaxes you?'

'Poetry does,' he said almost without thinking. 'Reading books on philosophy. Figuring out how things work. I have a curious mind and anything that engages it excites and relaxes me at the same time.'

'I'd like to know all about you,' she said. 'By the way, I haven't asked, and you haven't told me: What is it that you do?'

'I finished my engineering degree at the University of Illinois a few years back, and now I'm working at the Bucyrus Erie company in Milwaukee. It makes huge semi-diesel engines, and I work in the foundry. I will be sent on a secondment to Fairbanks Morse in Beloit for six months. They make heavy earth-moving and digging equipment, and at the moment they're working in Sind, in north-western India, not far from where my family lives. They're building the Sukkur Barrage, a massive dam across the Indus River and channel its waters to irrigation canals. If I make a good impression in Beloit, they will send me to the Barrage site in India as their engineering specialist and advisor. Do you know either of these companies?' he asked.

'I do! My father is an attorney in Beloit, and he represents Fairbanks Morse. I live in Beloit.'

He couldn't keep the excitement out of his voice. 'Beloit?' he said. 'You live in Beloit? Maybe we can meet. Where do you live in Beloit?' he asked.

'On Chapin Street. It's the main street that runs into Beloit College. I'm at 1024 Chapin. Promise me you'll come and visit me when you are in Beloit?'

Already making plans...he suspected she was always mapping out what she wanted and how to get others on board.

He turned the conversation to a safer subject. 'Where did you learn to play the piano? You must be quite good if you're teaching others,' he said.

'I was taught by Alexander Raab. Have you heard of him?'

'No, I admit I'm totally illiterate when it comes to classical music. You play classical I take it? Not jazz or ragtime?'

She laughed. 'No, I only play classical music. I haven't much interest in ragtime. Sometimes I play jazz but only for myself. Maybe I'll play some for you.'

She looked to see if he had any visible reaction to this offer. Then, she continued: 'Maestro Raab is a brilliant piano teacher. He teaches at the Chicago Music School, and when he has too many students, he asks his pupils to teach them. He asked me to be a guest teacher at the school. So that's why I go to Chicago every week. And the Auditorium Hotel is linked to the Auditorium Hall where there are recitals and where I teach in a salon.'

The train had left the long Oakton curve and was now entering the Skokie Valley Route. Past the congested areas of the North Shore, it now ran, at speeds up to 86 miles per hour, on an arrow-straight double track for 26 miles down the valley. They both noticed the change in speed and knew that Chicago was fast approaching. The wind whistled through the cracks in the window, and the glasses on Steve's counter rattled.

Just then, the doors of the parlour car opened and two young men in dark suits entered. They looked casually at the couple then sauntered over to the counter to get their food. One of them turned around, stared at Raj, and muttered something under his breath to his friend. And, while it was meant for his companion's ears (or was it?), Raj and Louise heard it. So did Steve, who looked over with alarm.

The word 'Arab', with a pejorative sting to it, hung in the air.

Immediately, Louise raised her voice. 'You, there!' she said imperiously.

One of the men turned around and stared at her. He said, 'Me?'

'No,' she answered, 'I was talking to your uncouth friend. Come here,' she commanded.

The culprit came over, taken aback by the brashness of this woman. Before he could say anything, she announced, in a cutting voice, 'My friend here is a Sikh and not an Arab. He's from India. Don't you know anything? You'd better apologize to him and to me, don't you think?'

The young man fumbled for words, then finally said, 'Excuse me, Ma'am, but I didn't mean to offend anybody.'

'Well, you did.'

'Uh, um, oh, well I'm sorry, Sir, my mistake.' Without a word to anyone, he walked over to the door of the car and walked out. His companion looked over, looked back at Steve, and then left the car too.

Steve was grinning, 'Well done, Mrs Lutes.'

She leaned forward to take Raj's hands in her own. 'Are you all right?' she asked. 'I'm sorry about that.'

'No need to worry,' he said, 'I usually ignore them. Sometimes, though, when I'm in the mood, I'll challenge them to a fight. Unfortunately, no one ever takes me up on that.'

'There were two of them.'

'I grew up in a part of India which is as lawless as the Wild West used to be here. So, I'm used to wrestling and brawling.'

She noticed, suddenly, that his hands were, indeed, very large. Reaching further forward, she touched his upper arm, and, beneath the cheap suit, she felt his muscles and his corded forearms.

'I guess you could have taken them on,' was all she said as she leaned back.

'Well, that's enough excitement, don't you think?' she asked, but her blue eyes had dimmed because she knew otherwise.

His blood was racing, and there was enough residual adrenaline left in him that he did something quite bold for him. He reached forward and, with the palm of his hand, caressed her cheek, and said, 'Thank you for your help.'

She blushed a deep red and hastily drank a deep sip of her coffee.

For a moment, they looked at one another, saying nothing, not wishing for the moment to end.

They were, by now, entering the northern outskirts of Chicago. Both knew that journey's end was near. Not wanting to break their connection, they both started to speak at the same time: 'I'll…' he said.

'Will…' she had begun, and then they both laughed.

'You first,' he said.

'Oh, I was going to ask, will you come for dinner? I'd really like that!'

'Yes, of course. 6 p.m. at the Auditorium, and I'll ask for your room.'

'Yes, but look for me. I'll wait for you in the lobby. You will remember?'

He nodded and got up to leave a tip for Steve. Then he helped her up and, with his hands on the small of her back, guided her out of the parlour car to the baggage compartment where she identified her luggage to the porter. They went back to the nearest car where they sat side by side for the last few minutes.

On the platform, she turned and looked at him and gave a small wave.

There was, he noticed, a jaunty sway in her hips as she walked off with her portmanteau.

NINE

Chicago Gurdwara, 13 April 1927

His thoughts, as he exited the terminus, were still on the woman he had just met on the train. He looked for Bawa, waiting with the crowds outside the Roosevelt Road terminus for him. But then he saw him, standing beside his 1920 Ford Model T, waving frantically at him. The car was running, and he recognized its rusty frame and its worn tires. Time, he thought, for Bawa to get a new car.

'What were you thinking about? I had to get out of my car to get your attention. You know I'm not allowed to park here for long. And, it's raining in case you haven't noticed.' Bawa was saying all this to him even as he embraced him enthusiastically.

A few minutes later, they were headed for the gurdwara at Randolph and Wells, about fifteen minutes north. The car's tired wipers scraped and squealed away in a desperate effort to clear off the raindrops. At the gurdwara, their other friends were waiting just inside the door, sheltered from the rain that was now petering off.

The gurdwara was like all the others he had been to

in America: it was small, and the prayer room doubled as the langar room. They went inside in bare feet, and his friends who did not wear turbans covered their heads with their handkerchiefs. Seated cross-legged on the floors, they listened as the kirtan service came to an end. It was already well past 1 p.m. and the gurdwara timetable was running late. Not that it mattered to him: he had nowhere to go until six that evening.

As always, he was drawn into the familiar cadences of the kirtan and entered a deep trance-like state. In the small room, he was aware of people talking in low tones, people reciting the hymn along with the raagis, people fidgeting. But these commotions did not deter him from his mindful awareness of inner peace. As one hymn ended, he noticed the gurdwara's secretary signalling to the lead raagi to end the kirtan part of the service.

As the last hymn was being sung, many of the congregants joined in the singing. A short prayer, the *ardaas,* signalling the end of the service was chanted by all. It was time to distribute the parshad, the sweet made from equal parts of ghee, flour and sugar, and he and Bawa went up to help serve it. He was given a stainless-steel bowl filled with parshad and as he approached the seated congregants, they held out their two palms, cupped, to receive a handful.

When he finished, he went over to Bawa and said, 'Let's get the room ready for langar.'

They took out several fresh sheets from a closet, folded them lengthwise to a quarter of their width, and placed them in straight lines down the length of the hall. The congregation sat down on these sheets in rows.

They helped distribute plates and spoons. Then they, along with several other helpers, brought out small buckets filled with creamy black daal to serve onto the plates. Bhattacharji, his friend, asked for a larger helping and he smiled as he served him. 'Tasty stuff isn't it?' he said and Bhattacharji acknowledged it with a grin.

'This is the best daal dish I ever had. Nobody makes it like you Sikhs.'

Other helpers followed with baskets of freshly made phulkas. These were handed out, and the helpers all stood in a line next to the kitchen and kept an eye out for people who wanted extra helpings.

He sensed that there was an air of satisfied community in that small hall as people sat, shoulder to shoulder regardless of their backgrounds, eating the langar. Once the congregants had been served, the helpers sat down with their own plates.

Bawa and he joined their friends, and they were soon exchanging news and gossip. He was glad that he was among friends. Most were still looking for jobs after their degrees and worked odd part-time ones to stay afloat. He wondered if he was going to tell them about meeting a very beautiful woman on the train but decided that he would not.

Sitting next to Bawa, he could not, however, hide his excitement about having met Louise on the train and of their upcoming dinner. He was constantly glancing at his watch, the one his family had given him as a going-away gift, purchased with love from the West End Watch Co. in Quetta, on the main street of Bruce Road, a mile or so from Harikishen Road and his beautiful house. Time, he could see, was ticking towards 6 p.m. but awfully slowly, he felt.

Bawa leaned over to him and said, 'I've never seen you in such a good mood. You're usually very serious and studious. But today, you look different. You look animated and happy. What happened? Did you meet someone exciting on the train?'

Was he so obvious? Regardless, Raj chose to ignore it and said, 'I'm just happy to be here with all of you.'

Bawa winked at him. 'I'm sure we're all glad to be here, too.' With his left hand, he clapped him on the shoulder.

'There's something black in the lentils,' he said, translating '*Daal mein kuchh kaala hai*', a Hindi saying into literal English, indicating that something fishy and mysterious was going on.

Raj, meanwhile, continued to chew his food stoically and refrained from saying anything. He was afraid that something would trickle out and his friends would spend the next few hours quizzing him non-stop. He did not want that. He wanted his brief memory of her to be free of their snickering comments.

After he helped the others clean up the plates and put them away, the five of them decided they would go to a nearby café for coffee and dessert. Giuseppe's, across the street, was deserted. A sad-looking Italian was happy to see a crowd trooping into his café. They had steaming mugs of cappuccino and a rustic looking apple and pear crostata. The sun was trying to come out and soon they were all involved in loud talk about their jobs, their aspirations in America, the possibility of going back to India, the dearth of good jobs there and the politics of the British Raj in their native land.

He was never one to talk much about himself. He came from a famously laconic family and felt that his personal life was his very own.

Bhattacharji suddenly leaned over to him across the table and asked, 'Tell me, you work in a foundry where the work is dirty and other workers are required to wear a hard hat. How did you get permission not to wear one?'

He really did not want to get into this conversation because he knew, inevitably, where it would lead. Choosing his words carefully, he said, 'I got special permission from my bosses to wear it because of my religion. It does get dirty and I have to wash one almost every day.'

Randhawa, his other Sikh friend at the table, said, 'You must have been very persuasive because I had no such luck. In fact, I had to cut off my hair just so I could get interviews for jobs.'

'Yes,' chimed in Lahiri, 'And tell us how you pulled it off. It's difficult for us Indians just to be considered for a job. For you Sikhs, it must be even more difficult.'

He could feel himself stiffening with anger and Bawa, sitting next to him, felt it too. Under the table, he touched him lightly on his thigh.

He was able to relax a bit and said to Lahiri with a casual shrug of his shoulders, 'I knew that my company was interested in securing a contract in India to build the Sukkur Barrage. They need trained engineers there, whom they can trust. I told them that I could be their engineer on site. I also told them that my family was very influential in that part of India and that my home was in

Quetta not that far from Sukkur. My family could help them retain that contract. In fact, my boss, Mr Fykes, visited Sukkur and Quetta and met my brother. He knows I come from a well-connected, prominent family. He must have told the higher-ups that I could help them there. I also told them that my family would reject me if I cut off my hair. So, I guess they bought it and let me keep my turban. My bosses have also been very appreciative of my work and my work ethic, so they have no complaints on that front.'

Lahiri nodded and sat back, convinced by the answer.

Bhattacharji, however, was not having any of this.

'Why don't you cut off your hair? You wouldn't have to wear a turban and you'd look like everyone else. You're a Sikh and you're all so fair-skinned, you'd pass for a southern European easily, maybe an Italian. Why not?'

This, of course, was the hidden question Raj knew was going to be asked. No matter how many times he had talked to them about it, they always persisted in asking this question. It made him angry.

Bawa intervened, 'Come on, Bhattacharji, we've been over this a million times. Why keep asking this? By the way, I wanted to ask you about your car, it's an Essex, isn't it? What do you think of it? Do you like it? How is the ride? I'm thinking of changing my car.'

The others at the table kept silent. They were relieved that Bawa, once again, had diverted them from going over the cliff.

But Raj was not having any of this. He was inwardly fuming.

'You know, no American I know, in school or at work,

has ever asked me to cut off my hair. But every non-Sikh Indian I know has asked me to do that. Why? Why must I look like you or anyone else?'

Bhattacharji was back-pedalling furiously, 'No, no, I was just asking. Just suggesting. Just trying to be funny. My God, you're always so argumentative and ready to fight!'

Bawa put his hand on him to restrain him from a further onslaught at Bhattacharji. 'By the way, did I tell you what happened to me at my office the other day?' he said.

Bawa's diversionary tactics had no effect on him.

'Tell me,' Raj said, still glowering at Bhattacharji, 'after the engineering degree you got, how come you haven't been able to find a job whereas I got one even before I graduated? You're so full of contempt for the Americans and so caught up in your own high-caste status that you refuse to do anything with your hands. You think they care? You're just a name and a number to them: you either want to work or you don't. It does not matter a jot to them.'

Now Bhattacharji was agitated because he had touched on a sore subject. He leaned forward to confront him, but Randhawa intervened, 'Hey, look, we're all friends, right? We're here to celebrate our New Year. We just listened to hymns of peace. We just had a great lunch. Free, too!' And he winked at them.

'Isn't this pie great?' exclaimed Lahiri. 'I'd like a refill of my coffee. Anyone else?' He signalled to the owner for more coffee.

Nobody said anything. The joviality had been replaced by tension.

Raj realized he had contributed to this atmosphere and, besides, was he angry at Bhattacharji? He was a well-meaning sort. What bothered him more were his own self-doubts about the turban and its necessity. He had had these internal arguments with himself many times before. Yes, he stood out but most of the time, he didn't care.

As though he were answering his own questions, he said in a more relaxed and explanatory manner, 'The turban is such a non-issue that there's no point in discussing it. I wear it because that is the way I see myself: this is my self-identity. If I were to look into the mirror and I was not wearing a turban, I would not recognize myself. It has zero to do with my values. It's just an integral part of my self-image. It hasn't been a hindrance and, if anything, has helped me differentiate myself. Besides, I learned very quickly that what matters here is your ability and desire to work, your drive to learn, and your ambition to excel. If you can add value, you'll be amply compensated. That is the American dream, after all, to improve one's lot, to leap economic levels, to achieve status based on one's honest efforts.'

In the quiet that followed, Raj felt he had been a bit too harsh with Bhattacharji. He was irked though that he was being pulled down to Bhattacharji's angst.

To lighten the mood around the table, he joked, 'In fact, it may help your career if you also put on a turban. I could help you with that and, if you did, I'm sure I could get you a job at the foundry.'

Everyone at the table laughed at that ridiculous statement and the moment of tension passed.

Before things could get grim again, Bawa, ever the

comedian, proceeded to crack a joke. 'What did the three Americans say when they went into a tea shop in Delhi and ordered three cups of tea? Why, cha-cha-cha, of course,' and chortled at his own joke.

They all laughed at this and Bhattacharji also gave an appreciative pat on Bawa's back. 'Tell us some more jokes, please. It's always good to laugh.'

Time passed quickly after that as they traded jokes, some crude, some not, some funny, some flat. He looked at his watch and saw that it was already 5 p.m.

Bawa saw him and said, 'Don't worry. I'll get you to the Roosevelt terminus in enough time for you to catch the train back.'

'You aren't going back to Milwaukee tonight, are you? Stay the night at my place,' insisted Bhattacharji. 'I'll make you a fine Bengali dinner of fish and rice!'

'No, I have to get back. I must get to work tomorrow since I took today off,' he said, knowing full well that what he really wanted to do was to have dinner with her.

'Oh, all right, another time then,' and Bhattacharji patted him on his back.

'Well, shall we find out the damage and pay our bill?' Randhawa suggested.

They divided the bill and paid their share, Bhattacharji insisting that he pay a double share. 'For my brother whom I think I insulted. I'm very sorry for what I said. And you're right, I must leave behind my prejudices and accept the ways here. I hope we can remain friends forever.'

In the car on the way back Bawa turned to him and grinned, 'I thought you were in a lighter mood. But you really chewed out Bhattacharji. You know, I cut off my hair a long time ago and all it has done for me is made me feel miserable for my weakness. I haven't had any more opportunities than you have and the few I had, I didn't seize. Unlike you. You're not concerned about doing anything. I admire that.'

'Well, don't be. Yes, I would like a better and more professional job. But I have firm belief in my God and that he will always take care of me and show me the right path.'

'There you go with your God stuff. Where do you get your belief from?'

'I don't know. I know that in my innermost being, I'm a Sikh.'

'Don't tell me that's because Guru Nanak himself asked an ancestor of yours that his eldest son be raised as a Sikh. You told me that story. Whether it's true or not, this belief, in God as provider, runs deep in you,' Bawa said. 'I hope he continues to provide for you and maybe you can put in a good word for me too. But you work hard to make opportunities for yourself, I've noticed.'

'Yes,' Raj replied, 'I think you've got it: I take every opportunity and make the most of it. That's my philosophy. If I'm working in the foundry, I want to be the best foundry man they've ever had. And if they send me to Sukkur, I'll be the best engineer they ever hired. That's my personal philosophy. Learn rigorously and be the best at whatever you do.'

By then they had reached the NSL station and Bawa parked his car at the curb. He turned, facing him, and said, 'Brother, I always feel humbled by your vision and your discipline. Doesn't all this drain you?'

'On the contrary,' Raj said, 'it energizes me. I realize that I don't know much. My curious mind drives me to learn more. And, as I learn, I realize I know less and less. And that drives me further.'

'And how far will you go? When do you stop learning?'

'Ah, that's easy: when I'm dead! As a Sikh, we are enjoined to be students forever. You know that that is what the word "Sikh" means, right? I feel that if we stop learning, we stop growing and when we stop growing, we might as well be dead. And that word, in a sense, defines me and drives me into being an integral Sikh. That is, I am one with the philosophy.'

'God save us from your lectures,' Bawa said with a laugh. 'You're twenty-eight and I already feel sorry for your wife to be, your children to come and your future friends: they'll be captives for your discourses, won't they?'

Raj, too, had to laugh. Sometimes, he thought, I'm too serious for my own good. I need to shed that mantle and be able to play as well. Perhaps, he thought, I will have that opportunity.

With that, he hugged Bawa, wished him well and promised to get together soon.

As soon as Bawa had left, Raj turned northwards and began walking briskly towards the Auditorium. The rain had chilled the temperature and he turned up his suit collar and strode, at a brisk pace, on the rain-soaked pavement. As he settled into a rhythm he realized again how much he loved to walk and how much he valued physical activity. It steadied his mind into a peaceful trance.

TEN

Chicago, The Auditorium Hotel, 13 April 1927

He walked up State Street for a block, then cut east on 11th Street to South Michigan Avenue. This way he would skirt Grant Park and meet West Congress Parkway in about five blocks, where the Auditorium stood.

At 7th Street, he saw the almost completed hulk of a huge building occupying the entire block on South Michigan. A lit-up sign announced the opening of the Stevens Hotel in May of that year. He stopped for a moment and counted the floors: Twenty-six! Amazing.

Past East Harrison Street, the large tower of the Auditorium came into view. He could see now that it would be dwarfed by the new Stevens Hotel. He looked at his watch. It was a few minutes to six, and he did not want to be early. So, he walked past the grand entrance of the Auditorium and turned left on East Harrison Street, finding another way to get in.

Inside the hotel, the marbled, carpeted expanse of the lobby spread out before him. It evoked elegance and wealth, and, for an instant, he felt under-dressed in his ill-fitting suit.

He looked around for Louise but didn't see her at first. Then he did, and his breath caught in his throat. She was seated on one of the armchairs facing the main entrance, dressed in a sleeveless black silk dress with gilded lace accents. The lace formed a long scarf along the front of the dress, and was held at the waist by a large, square brooch with a black stone set in the middle. Around her neck was a long strand of pearls that ended at her waist. She was, to him, grace and beauty personified.

Louise was sitting straight up but leaning forward a bit. Her eyes, fixed on the doors, were alive with eagerness. A small smile hovered on her lips. Her entire body was relaxed, but at the same time tense with anticipation. He sensed her excitement, and it sent a spark through him.

As he approached her, she must have felt his presence for she turned and gave him a dazzling smile.

'Ah! There you are. And right on time. I like a punctual man. Poor dear, but you look a bit cold. Where's your overcoat? Are you all right?'

'I'm fine,' he said, shrugging off her concern. 'Have you seen all the construction on Michigan? There's a brand new hotel coming up, and its twenty-six storeys. I counted them!'

'Yes, I have, and they did approach me, you know. They know I'm a long-term resident of this hotel, but they were enticing me with special rates. But I feel loyal to the Auditorium,' she said, with the same flirting twinkle in her eyes he'd seen earlier.

'Loyal?'

'Oh yes. After I started staying here, the Auditorium management asked if I were going to be a regular visitor and I said yes. I told them I taught piano next door at the music school, and they immediately offered me a long-term apartment. It's available whenever I want it—like a small pied-à-terre, you know. It's just one bedroom and a sitting room, but it has a lovely view of the park and the lake, and I got a good deal on it. It even has a little fireplace which the maid lights for me on cold days. In fact, there's a nice fire up in my room. Would you like to see it?'

She said this in an openly playful manner, leaning forward and touching him on the forearm, and he felt himself turn red.

'Oh, don't mind me,' she said, 'I didn't want to put you on the spot. Just teasing! But, if you want, we can go upstairs, and then go to the dining room: It's on the top floor of the hotel, and they serve lovely meals made by French chefs. When I'm here, I take all my meals there. They even have a special table for me. Shall we go? Are you hungry?'

He wasn't particularly hungry, but he didn't want to make her wait. Besides, he wanted to catch the 8 p.m. train back to Milwaukee.

'Yes, sure,' he said. 'Let's go see your room and then we can eat. But is it OK for me to go up?'

She waved away the question as though it were a pesky fly. 'Usually the management is strict about male visitors in a lady's apartment. But I told that young Mr Johnson, the manager, that it was the most Victorian thing I had ever heard. I mean, this is my second home, and I should be able to invite anyone I choose to visit me. He shrank away when I said that! Anyway, he's allowed me to take anyone I want to my rooms.'

He held out his hand to help her up, and she took it eagerly. He noticed, again, that she had long fingers. A pianist's hands.

She stood up and put her arm through his, and they walked towards the elaborate elevators. Several eyes followed them: an elegant, beautiful woman with an exotic-looking man.

~

The elevator had gilded doors with images of a Caesar-like king, with a crown of wreaths, and his queen, with a garland of flowers. Above the doors was a gilded, semi-circular floor indicator with a large arrow.

As they stepped in, the attendant touched his cap and said, 'Good evening, Mrs Lutes. Are you going to your room or to the dining room?'

'My room, John,' she said.

'Right away, Mrs Lutes,' he said. Inside the elevator were mirrors in elaborate gilded frames. Louise looked at herself and patted her hair to make sure it was in place.

Riding up in silence, he was aware of her perfume, a light floral mix that hinted of roses. It reminded him of the attar of roses he had bought for his mother just before he left India. He and Louise were looking straight ahead at the attendant's back, but out of the corner of his eye, he noticed her glancing at him sideways. She smiled and intertwined her fingers in his.

'Here's 16, Mrs Lutes,' the attendant announced and stepped aside to let them out.

'Will you be dining later?' he asked.

'Yes, we will, John,' she replied, 'and I'll ring for the elevator.'

'I'll come right up, Mrs Lutes.'

'Well, here we are, Raj,' she said. 'My apartment is down there at the end.' They were in a wide corridor with thick grey-green carpeting, the walls covered in light yellow wallpaper with geometric designs.

She came to a stop at the last door, number 1602, and extracted a key from her clutch. Inside, he got a whiff of her heady perfume mixed with the woodsy aroma of pine logs from the fireplace. All the lights were on and, through the fluttering curtain at the double-width window across from the door, he could see the lights around the Buckingham Fountain in the park.

'Come, let me show you around,' she said. One of the windows was slightly open, and she pushed down the sash to shut it. A slight shiver went through her. 'I forgot I had left the window open. A little cold, don't you think?'

Instinctively, he put his arms around her shoulder, and, without any hesitation, she drew into his embrace. He was acutely aware of her luminous skin, the blue of her eyes, her lustrous hair.

'You're warm,' she said.

He nodded. 'I'm always warm.'

A moment later, she slipped out of his arms and gesturing around the room said, 'What do you think?'

He looked around reluctantly. All he wanted was to look at Louise. But he was anxious about showing his hunger for her.

'I'm very lucky,' Louise said. 'I have a corner apartment, so I have a lot of windows and light. Look,' she went on. 'I even have a tiny kitchen. It's all wasted, really, because I hate to cook, and when I try, the results are always disastrous. There I go! What a silly woman: trying to impress a handsome man I've just met and the first thing I tell him is I can't cook!'

He was turning to her when she took his hand and said, 'Come look at the bedroom.'

Noticing his unease, she laughed. 'Oh, come now, you're not afraid of little old me, are you? Come on,' she said, tugging at him.

As they walked in, he put his arms around her, and she moved closer into him. 'Look at the two of us,' she said, pointing to the mirror above the make-up table, 'I see a tall, handsome, virile man standing next to me.'

'And I see a beautiful goddess next to him…'

This time, they both laughed. She pointed to a small door on the right side of the bed. 'That leads to the bathroom. Why don't you make yourself comfortable, and I'll be out in a second?'

She disappeared.

He noticed that the fire in the sitting room needed attention. Almost every room in their rambling house in Quetta had a fireplace, and he liked tending them. Two fat, bronze andirons held a few burning logs. There were French fleur-de-lis designs on the andirons and matching ones on the handles of the tools next to the fireplace. He selected the poker and tongs and set about rearranging the logs so they burned brighter. He also added a log from a pile behind the tools.

Standing up he noticed the silver framed photographs on the mantle—pictures of a young boy and a girl, and another of an older couple.

A third, casual photograph showed Louise with the two teenage children and the same older couple, as well as a second man. This was an odd grouping. Louise, at the left end of the image, was in a short-sleeved, dark coloured sheath with a pleated bottom and pearl buttons down the length of the dress. Next to her was the teenage boy, smiling broadly at the camera. The young girl, also wearing a short-sleeved dark sheath, was in front of the boy. Next to them was the older couple: The woman, severe-looking in a dress that reached her ankles, was turned slightly to her right so that her left shoulder pointed towards the camera. She had a calculating look in her eyes that Raj decided was particularly flinty. The older man next to her, in a dark jacket and vest with grey trousers, wore spectacles and a hat; a fob watch was tucked into the upper pocket of his vest. He was tall and pot-bellied, with a white goatee. Facing the older woman, he had his back almost completely turned to the other man in the image. That man, on the right end of the group, was perhaps in his forties, already with a receding hairline; he had a puzzled, bemused look on his face—almost of exasperation. The older couple was turned away from him, as if they were mentally trying to deny his presence. All of them, except the odd man out on the right, were squinting into the bright sun.

'There you are,' she said as she came into the room. She looked refreshed, and a new dab of perfume preceded her. A light woollen stole was draped across her shoulders.

'You've met them?' she asked, pointing to the photos. 'My family; I'll tell you all about them over dinner. Shall we go?'

ELEVEN

Chicago, The Auditorium Hotel restaurant, 13 April 1927

When they got to the dining room, the maître d'hôtel, done up in an impossibly elegant black dinner jacket, glided over. His black hair was pomaded and brushed back to a shine.

'Ah! Mrs Lutes! What a pleasure to see you again! I'll tell Henri you are dining with us! I'm sure he'll make you his best dish.'

'Thank you, Charles,' she said. 'My friend is from India. He's an engineer, and he's dying to have Henri's roast mutton. Aren't you, darling?' she added flashing her dazzling smile and blue eyes at him. If he was rattled by her choice of endearment, he hid it well.

'Bien sûr, Madame!' Charles beamed at him. 'Please follow me,' he said as he led them to a private table far away from the other diners.

The dining room seemed to stretch out forever. There were rows of tables geometrically placed down the length of the room. Potted palms separated the tables.

Charles had led them to the table furthest away from

the entrance and away from most of the occupied tables. 'Oh no, Charles! This won't do at all,' Louise admonished him. 'You're banishing us to the suburbs here. I want my usual table.'

'I'm so sorry, Madame, I thought the two of you would want to be private.' His eyes lingered over Raj, uneasily, taking in his beard and turban.

Behind them, a few diners stared not only at the odd-looking man but also at the tableau: the courteous maître d', the exotic foreigner, and the beautiful, imperious woman. The diners at the nearest table caught themselves staring and hastily looked down at their plates.

He led them to another table almost at the centre of the dining room but set against a large window.

'Here we are, Madame, your table. I'm going to send Frederick over to wait on you, tout de suite.'

With that, Charles snapped his fingers and their waiter, Frederick, came hurrying over with leather-bound menus. He was a short African-American man dressed in a white jacket, black trousers, and a black bow tie. He stood proudly straight, seeming taller than he was.

'Good evening, Mrs Lutes! Good evening, Sir! Welcome to our dining room.' Frederick then described the specials—which included roast mutton—and asked if they wanted something to drink.'

Raj turned towards her: 'What will you have?'

'Oh, I'm in the mood to celebrate! A dry Martini for me, Frederick.'

'Water's fine for me,' Raj said.

'Dry Martini?' Raj asked once Frederick was gone. 'Isn't there a Prohibition going on?'

'Well of course there's a Prohibition going on. But, you know, everything is available…for a price.'

'And what are you celebrating with that drink?' he ventured.

This time she firmly clasped his hand: 'But, of course, it's you, darling. It's us. A new beginning. Wherever this takes us.'

He flushed with pleasure. Yet, he knew he was being seduced and would have to tread carefully.

Leaning back in his chair, he opened the red leather-bound menu with 'The Auditorium' emblazoned in gold on the cover and his eyes popped. The prices were astronomical. He mentally went through his wallet to figure out how much he had. He was becoming increasingly uncomfortable—the damn tie was suddenly knotted too tightly, and the wool of his trousers, even though it had worn thin, was beginning to itch.

She noticed how he was running his finger between his neck and his collar and the slight reddening of his cheeks. She touched him lightly on the hand, 'Don't let these prices shock you, darling.'

Again, 'darling': did she call everyone that?

'Oh, no, they're quite reasonable. No, I suddenly felt a little warm. Don't you think it's warm here?'

She gave a little shrug of her shoulders and smiled at him.

'I have special pricing here since I'm a long-term resident. What I pay is nowhere near what you see. Dinner is a dollar for me no matter what I eat. Also, it's my treat tonight in celebration of our friendship. And, by the way, I guessed you like mutton, so I suggest you have it.' And she held up her hands to shush away his protestations.

Eventually, he saw he could not make much progress with this headstrong woman. He relented and said, 'OK, just this once. But, in the future, I'll pay.'

She gave him a mock salute and laughed. 'Oh, I'm going to have fun with you, aren't I?'

Somewhat relieved yet peeved for a reason he did not totally understand, he sat back and looked around the dining room.

And then it came to him. Out of his past, the Pashto word *ghairat.* In the language of the Pathans of his native Quetta, it identified the singular ability of a man to make sure all his responsibilities were fulfilled. To look after those who were his family. To feed, protect, and care for them.

Immediately he stopped. She wasn't family, but he felt a strong bond with her. Still, he needed to slow down, he thought to himself: This is going too fast. He'd promised his family in India he would work after he got his engineering degree to earn his passage back home, and then help raise his younger siblings. But he could stay here for a while...couldn't he?

'...Oh, there you are!' Louise cried. 'For a moment I thought I had lost you! I was saying, isn't this a nice room, but you were miles away.'

He now looked around at the room.

It was enormous, long and rectangular, with a high, barrel-vaulted ceiling. The room was heavily carpeted, and drapes hung on all the windows.

'Louis Sullivan was the architect in case you're

wondering. My mother knew Louis quite well when she was in New York. He's the one responsible for these awfully high buildings sprouting in Chicago. Pity he did not live to see his dream of skyscrapers dominating the skyline. He died only a few years ago.'

'Yes, we learned about him in engineering school. Remarkable.'

Frederick appeared with their drinks, and she clinked her cocktail glass with his water glass, saying, 'Here's to a long and deep friendship. Well, that hits the spot. I had a late night yesterday. Really, people impose on me, you know.'

He did not say anything, just looked at her inquiringly. By now, he knew she would tell him what was on her mind, whether he asked or not.

'I gave a small concert last night. I compose classical music, and give concerts and lectures. I told you I also tutor pupils in music. Well, last night I did a little concert and lecture in Beloit. Afterwards, six people from the audience followed me back to the studio and stayed quite late.'

Once again, she sensed his mind had wandered. 'You know, you have a mysterious way of disappearing into that head of yours,' she said with a laugh. 'Here I am trying to make an impression on you and you're…where?'

'My apologies,' he said. 'It's just that, as an engineer, I was trying to figure out how this building was constructed. Fascinating. Oh, and you don't have to make an impression on me—I'm impressed by you. I'd like to know you better but, in a way, I feel I know you already. I feel at ease with you.'

'Darling! That's so nice to hear. I must confess that when I saw you, I was immediately taken. Yes, I saw you peeking at me from the train window. And then, I was hoping you'd show up in the parlour car. And you did! It's destiny, you know. Don't you agree, Raj?'

'I'm not a great believer in destiny, or *kismet,* as we call it. I think we make our own destiny.'

Unbidden, a couplet from Iqbal came into his head:

Make yourself so powerful that
Before proscribing your destiny
God Himself will ask you
Tell me, what is it you desire?

This, though, was not the time to recite poetry. Instead, he leaned forward and stroked her hand: 'I was drawn to you immediately, too. Maybe our paths crossed by coincidence but, then again, I believe things happen for a reason. We have to discern what those seeming coincidences mean.'

'Okay, my Wise-Man-From-the-East, we'll figure it out later. But, first, let's order dinner.'

'Have you made your choices, Mrs Lutes? Sir?' Frederick stood ready to take their order.

'Raj, are you ready?' He nodded but deferred to her.

'Well, then, Frederick, I'm going to have the soup and the trout,' she said.

'I'll just have the roast mutton, please,' he said. 'Tell me about the people in the photograph,' he said once Frederick departed.

'They're my family. The older couple are my parents. My father is an attorney as I told you, a very well-known one. My mother comes from a rich family that was one of the benefactors of Beloit College. The two teenagers are my children. I have a son, John, and a daughter, Josephine.'

'And the other man?' he asked.

'You get right to the point, don't you? I'm very direct too, as you're getting to know. His name is Frank, but everyone calls him Shorty. We got married when I was young. I fell in love with this cavalier Canadian, and my parents were dead set against him. They thought he was a wanderer and a vagabond. They weren't wrong, I found out. But too late. They sent me away to school in New York so I would be far away from him. But I did what every girl in love does: I rebelled and married him. To make sure I was taken care of, my parents insisted we live in the same house as them.

'It's a two-storey, eighteen-room house on Chapin Street. We lived on the upper floor while my parents occupied the ground floor. Things worked out well for a few years. Then I found out he was having an affair. We got divorced. He still lives in Beloit, though, and I'm still with my parents.'

'Is that how you can get away every week to Chicago—your mother takes care of your children while you're away?'

'I'd be the first to say that I'm a dreadful mother. I adore my children. But I can't cook and clean. We have dinner downstairs with my parents, even when I'm there. My mother is more of a mother to her grandchildren than I am. I don't think there will be any disagreements as to my capabilities as a mother. Do you think I'm dreadful? Ignoring my children for my own pursuits?'

Beneath her self-assured manner, he sensed a well of vulnerability. He reached across and squeezed her arm. 'I'm sure you're doing the best you can,' he reassured her.

She put her hand on his and said, 'Thanks. That means a lot to me.'

Frederick arrived with their main course, and Raj ate with gusto. The mutton was reminiscent of the lamb rogan josh his mother cooked, which was his favourite dish. The way she made it, the lamb was so tender, it fell off the bones. The sauce was always a deep reddish-brown, redolent with traditional spices from Kashmir: whole cinnamon, black peppercorns, black and green cardamom, fennel seeds, bay leaves and a special red pepper that gave the dish its deep red hue, but was not hot. He would have that dish with fresh phulkas spread with homemade butter. The thought made his eyes water.

'Are you OK?' she asked. 'You look like you're having an orgasm!'

He almost choked on a tender piece of mutton. She really was a plain-spoken, earthy woman.

'Yes, I'm fine. Just remembering home cooking.'

She laughed outright. 'Well, I won't be adding to your memories on that score since I don't cook. But I can give you other memories...' Once again, that look.

When they finished, Frederick asked if they wanted dessert. She said no but Raj ordered apple pie à la mode.

He ate slowly, as was his custom, aware that she was watching him closely. When she touched his leg under the table with her foot, he looked up, startled, but quickly smiled and went on with his pie.

'You seem to be content with yourself,' she said. 'But do you ever wonder what others think of you? Just sitting here, I can't help but notice that people are looking at you surreptitiously. You stand out with your beard and turban. Does it make you uncomfortable?'

She had touched on a sore point. 'Yes, I am aware sometimes that people stare at me. Someone like you with me is bound to stoke curiosity. I pass it off as ignorance.'

'But if you're uncomfortable, even if only sometimes, why don't you do something about it?'

'Like what? This morning on the train, you intervened. I told you I could have taken care of those two people in the car. But you chased them off. Did my presence make you uncomfortable? Are you uncomfortable now?'

'I'm feeling a bit prickly because of the way people are looking at us. I'm uncomfortable but it's because of you, of how I think you may be feeling.'

'I'm fine. There's nothing I can or want to do to change my appearance. I must live with it or I'd go under with all that scrutiny. I'm not going to allow others to stop me living the way I want.'

'I want you to know that I love the way you look and carry yourself. There's a lot of dignity in your aura and I am very attracted to that.' She leaned forward and stroked his beard.

'OK, now,' he blushed. 'I'm not used to that much of an open display of affection in public. Maybe we can save that for a more private time.'

'Oh, we can save a lot of other things for private times!'

By now they were both done with their coffees.

Frederick came over and said, 'I've put this on your account, Mrs Lutes. Is that OK?'

She nodded. Raj got up and helped her from her chair. At his station, Charles bid them good night.

'Please come back soon, Mrs Lutes,' he said, bowing. 'And, Sir, you too! Please come back. Au revoir!'

In the elevator, John was waiting to take them down one floor.

When they stepped out on her floor, she quickly turned and surprised him with a kiss on his mouth. Then she put her arms around his waist, her head on his shoulders and they sauntered down to 1602. He casually draped his arms around her and felt the curve of her hips.

When they entered the room, he shut the door and, without a word, picked her up in his arms and headed towards the bedroom.

She nestled into his chest.

TWELVE

Beloit, Wisconsin, June 1927

When Raj reached Chapin Street, he paused for a few moments before continuing. He had walked from the Beloit train station at his usual brisk pace. But now, he wanted to compose himself before meeting Louise in the house he knew she shared with her parents.

It had been a tumultuous few months since they'd met on the train. They saw each other regularly, mostly at the Auditorium Hotel in Chicago and her apartment there. Sometimes, though, she had visited him in South Milwaukee in the room he rented. That had proved to be awkward for him, and they decided not to anymore. Now, for the first time, he was going to her home in Beloit.

'We live separately,' she had explained when he asked about her living arrangements. 'My parents live on the ground floor, and my children and I live on the upper floor. My teaching studio is there too.'

'How private is the upstairs part?' he had asked.

'What you're asking, Raj, I think, is will anyone disturb us there.'

He turned a bright red, and she giggled, 'Of course not.'

As he approached her house, he saw two young girls playing hopscotch on the pavement. Both fell silent when they saw him. He was about to ask if Louise lived at that address when he heard the front door open.

She stood on the stoop, looking down at him and the two girls. Without a word, she held out her hand waving him in. She hustled him up the stairs to her studio. It was only behind closed doors that they embraced and kissed.

'You know, when I saw you at the gate, you looked very aloof and detached,' Louise told him.

'Did I?' Raj said. 'I must have been trying to put on an act for the children. Is one of them your daughter?'

'Yes, the one with the short hair is my daughter, Jo. The other is her best friend, Marjorie. I hope that was an act: as you walked up the path to the door you looked as cold as an iceberg. I thought, he's come to tell me it's all off.'

He laughed. 'No, just an act as I told you.'

'Would you like some tea?' she asked.

He nodded yes, and she went off to make it. Louise's studio was, in fact, a suite of rooms in the front of the house, set apart from her bedrooms by a central hallway. In the corner of the studio was what he thought must be a salon grand piano; the metal plate said it was made by Chickering in 1925. There was an adjustable bench in front of the piano as well as a chair next to it where, he assumed, she sat when teaching. On a long table, near the piano, was a stack of music sheets, some brochures, and a metronome. There were two armchairs, as well as plain, straight-backed wooden chairs that were arranged around the walls. He counted twenty and guessed they would be arranged in rows for concerts.

At one end of the studio, large French glass doors led to a sunny sitting room, elegantly furnished with deep sofas and armchairs upholstered in a light-yellow fabric. At the far end of the sitting room was a large marble-mantled fireplace. There were many photographs on the mantel, mostly of Louise and her family.

He wandered into the bedroom and saw a little pillow, nestled among the larger ones. Picking it up, he was aware of her heady aroma. He kissed it.

Louise, entering at that moment, saw him and laughed. 'Oh, look who's sentimental now, and how often have you told me you're not sentimental? But, Raj, that marvelous sixth sense of yours somehow told you just which pillow lies beneath my cheek at night. Why do you deny you are sentimental, dearest? You may not be about some things but with me you have always been deeply romantic, and I love that in you!'

Raj, embarrassed again, put the pillow back on the bed and shrugged.

'Let's sit down in the studio and have tea,' Louise declared. 'I brought you some shortbread cookies—the ones that you like. Also, I want to show you something.'

She picked up a few brochures from the table next to the piano and sat beside Raj on one of the sofas facing the fireplace. She gave him a folded four-page brochure, which featured a photograph of her on the front, looking quite serious. The inside two pages listed her many musical services, while the last page displayed endorsements from leading musicians in the area.

'Is this a brochure you use to advertise your musical services?'

Louise Rood Lutes

Presents a Series of Talks on

Musical Appreciation

Illustrated at the Piano

Everyone loves music but there are many people who for fear of the bugbear "classical" music, under which title they place all forms with which they are unfamiliar, shun concerts and operas that would bring them the keenest enjoyment, if they could but listen with understanding.

It is to this class, or even those who have devoted some time to serious study, that Louise Rood Lutes comes as a friendly counsellor, with her sound musical advice, her delightful interpretations at the piano, and last but not least, her attractive manner of presentation.

It is not possible to hear her without receiving the key to better enjoyment of the kind of music with which she deals, and a glance at her list of topics will establish the scope and value of her work.

TOPICS

A Brief Glance at the History of Music Composition.

The Ancestry of the Pianoforte.

An Outline of Music History. (Five Lecture-Recitals.)

Certain periods in Music Compared with kindred Eras in Dress. (Illustrated also with paintings.)

A Glimpse of American Music.

Some Modern Questions in Composition.

Special topics to suit the needs of Clubs will be prepared on notice of from six weeks to two monhts.

'Yes, it is. I hate that photo, though. My agent, Maude Rea, had it taken in a studio by a professional photographer, and she said I needed to strike a serious pose. Took some effort on my part, I'll tell you.'

'You're always laughing and making faces. I bet it *was* difficult.' Raj paused, then added, 'I don't like it. You're much more beautiful. But look at what you're advertising,' he continued. 'Lectures on music and musicology, piano lessons, concerts, talks on period instruments. This is deep stuff, to me, at least. You just introduced me to western classical music, but now I see you know so much more.'

'Why, Mr Singh, I'm shocked, that sounds so condescending...so *male.*'

Startled, he turned to her and said, 'You know I'm not that way. My mother made us understand that women are equal to men in all respects and, by the way, that is the philosophy of my religion as well. Did you know that some women led Sikh armies?'

'You see what you do? I was joking, a least a little, and you turn all serious. You're always spouting philosophy.'

She smiled, signalling that she'd been teasing, and handed him another brochure.

'This is sheet music, published by G. Schirmer, Inc., New York, in 1924, of my compositions entitled *Two Descriptive Pieces—Coquette and Aunt Mandy Sings.*'

He looked at the music. 'On page one of Coquette, your direction, as a composer, is that the piece should be played, "Not rapidly, but in a capricious mood". What does that mean?'

'I mean to play it impulsively. It shouldn't seem that the music was composed. Rather, it just came to the player. Yes, I can't be serious for too long. Even my composition must be taken with a pinch of salt.'

'I wish I could hear the music.'

No sooner had he said it, than she began playing the piece. He closed his eyes and let the music fill his head. When she finished, he clapped and went over to hug her. 'Thank you for sharing that with me.'

TWO DESCRIPTIVE PIECES

For the Piano

By

LOUISE ROOD LUTES

—*Coquette*

Aunt Mandy Sings

Price, each, 25 cents, net
(In U.S.A.)

G. SCHIRMER, INC., NEW YORK

'One day, I'll compose a piece of music for my man.' With that, she kissed him. 'Look at this other brochure.'

There was a list of ten junior students who had recently played their practiced pieces at a recital, on 4 February 1927, at 7:30 p.m. A second list included eight senior students who played their pieces on Saturday, 5 February 1927, also at 7:30 p.m. 'I wish I could come to one of these performances,' he mused.

'Yes, I'd like that, Raj. But, for now, maybe you can come to Scoville Hall at Beloit College where I give larger recitals.'

'We must keep this thing between us a secret: is that what you're saying? In the hall, I'd just be a spectator.'

'Yes, darling, for the time being. Don't you agree?'

'Tell me more about the pianoforte and your musical history talks,' he said, attempting to steer the conversation to safer topics.

'Why don't I tell you about my gowns, instead? Much more interesting. Let me show you.'

With that, Louise jumped up and went into the bedroom, returning with several gowns draped over her arm.

'How many do you have?' Raj asked.

'I like to have a new gown for every formal recital.'

'You must have quite a few then.'

'Not exactly. When I get tired of one, I sell it off.'

'To whom?'

'Oh, just this week for instance, I sold one to the wife of J. Forsythe Crawford, who is professor of psychology and human behaviour at Beloit College, down the road.'

'So, you know people there? Did you go to that college?'

'No. But we do know a lot of the professors there. I told you too that my mother's family, the Merrills, were one of the original funders of the college. 'But let's leave that story for another day,' Louise went on. 'Here, let me show you what these gowns look like on me.'

Without bothering to draw the curtains, she proceeded to strip off all her clothes, including her bra, and slipped on the first gown.

'I went down to my favourite store in Chicago on Monday and bought this very pretty taffeta dress. It feels like the same material as that Persian turban you gave me, darling, a rather heavy and stiff silk. Do you like the colour? See, it's peach.'

She came close to him and leaned down to kiss him. Then she turned around to show off the gown. It had narrow silver braids on the top and a soft pink covered with silver flowers on the skirt and waist.

'Do you like it?'

'The kiss? Of course, I like it.'

She gave him a little punch in the chest. 'I'm asking about the *gown.*'

'I love the colour, and I especially like the lemon-coloured parts on the skirt.'

'Just a moment. Let me show you the whole outfit.'

She put on a big black hat, which she slanted over her face, and slipped into shoes made of a very pale kid. Then she he sashayed around the room.

'You like?'

'Very much. Come here and I'll show you how much.'

'Oh no you don't. I have other gowns to show you.'

She shed her clothes again and proceeded to model several more gowns: all made of silk, all eye-catching.

While she was putting on her show, he was sipping tea and crossing and uncrossing his legs. At one point, he glanced quickly at his watch.

Louise noticed. 'My man is impatient. I wonder what he wants. Soon enough, darling. I do have one more thing to show you. It's an outfit for a dance. You have to promise you won't laugh.'

He crossed his heart.

She skipped out of the room and went back into the bedroom. When she returned, she stood at attention, and cleared her throat.

'Let me introduce this piece. There's a music club in Beloit called Treble Clef, where I give some of my lectures and recitals, you know. Well, they're going to put on a "stunt" afternoon, and they've asked me to do a Spanish Dance! So, I've come up with this rather fanciful costume which is more Egyptian than anything else, or maybe it's Turkish.' She paraded around in full harem trousers of blue silk, a green scarf around her waist, and a tight wrapping of silver gauze around her breasts.

She did a twirl as before. 'I like the bare tummy,' he offered.

'Of course, you would, darling. You'd like everything bare, wouldn't you? Anyway, my feet will be bare, though heavily-rouged, and my own hair will be covered with artificial dark braids. I'll be carrying a covered basket on my head. Like so,' she said, putting a small basket on her head.

'This is a basket woven by Native American Indians that my mother bought when we lived in Albuquerque, where my father was a leading lawyer. Also imagine that in that corner there will be a pedestal and a gramophone player on the pedestal. Okay ready?'

When he nodded, she went over to a corner and dragged out a wooden cart on wheels. The cart had a gramophone on it. She selected a small record from a shelf under the cart and placed it on the turntable.

'Naturally, I've written some zany music for this.'

'You recorded it as well?' he said, 'I'm amazed at all your talents.'

She started the gramophone and strange music quickly filled the air. It was vaguely familiar, and he was trying to place it but then she placed the basket on her head and started dancing.

To say it was an exotic dance would be an understatement. She was dancing around the room, imitating temple dancers in ancient Egypt, then whirling around like a dervish. Round and round the room she went, her harem pants flaring out with her movements. Suddenly, she turned and did a particularly good imitation of a belly dance—her torso shimmying, her hips grinding, her fingers snapping. From this, she went into a passably good simulation of an Indian classical dance with exaggerated hand gestures and eye movements, her feet tapping an incessant beat. The basket stayed firmly on her head but there was something rattling around in it. The music was building to a climax, when he realized it sounded like a gypsy tune with its origins in folk music from the Rajasthan area of northwest India.

He was clapping to the music. The dance, in keeping with the music, was also working up to a fever pitch, and she was swaying in front of the pretend pedestal, writhing, and weaving like a snake. She placed the basket on the piano top and bowed down in front of it as though it were an idol. Then she continued her frenetic dancing in time with the rising music. The dance now was flamenco style: her feet were stamping the ground emphatically and her hands clapping out a rhythm in time with the music. From time to time, she would snap her fingers and shout out 'Olé!'

Finally, the music reached a crescendo then crashed into silence. Moving swiftly, she whipped off the cover of the basket and took out a huge Spanish onion. She held it in front of her, in both hands, like some sacred object.

Turning to him with a flourish, she said, 'Voila. That's my Spanish Dance! Idiotic, but did you like it?'

She had collapsed onto him, laughing, her breast heaving with the energy expended, her skin glowing. He held her in a tight embrace.

'It's the best dance I've ever seen! And it's not idiotic. It's clever. I like the title—the Spanish Dance. I see how cleverly you tied the dance to a Spanish onion. Are you sure you won't shock the Treble Clef members with that costume?'

'I don't care. I'm going to have fun.'

She kissed him and held onto him for a long time.

'My man likes it. That's all I want to hear.'

She took his hand and led him into the bedroom.

Later, as she lay in his arms, she said. 'Do you think it would be better if I wore a wrap around my head, like a turban? It'll be more glamorous.'

He was getting a little bored with her incessant chatter, and said nothing. But she was up and putting on her costume again. Then she rummaged around her closet and came upwith a piece of peach-coloured heavy silk. 'Tie this around my head like a turban, would you?' she said to Raj. 'Let's see what it looks like.'

He willingly obliged. He made her stand facing him and then he pleated the silk into narrow, four-inch strips. He gave her one end of the long cloth to hold and proceeded to wrap the silk around her head.'

'You look beautiful,' he assured her 'The whole outfit suits you.'

'I feel beautiful, darling, and it's all because of you. You make me feel…desired and knowing that, makes me feel more beautiful. I love the turban. I may have to adopt it as a personal style gesture.'

She started twriling around the room again, though this time without the music. Raj joined in, performing the shoulder-popping, arms-aloft movements of the bhangra. The two whirled around the room until a tired Louise collapsed in his arms. Her chest was heaving, her eyes bright. She was, at that moment, the most attractive woman he had ever seen.

THIRTEEN

Chicago, The Auditorium Hotel, 13 August 1927

Raj never went back to the studio in Beloit again. However, he and Louise continued to see each other as often as they could.

On Saturday, 13 August, they arranged to have dinner at the Auditorium, then go to the Art Museum on Sunday. But Louise explained she'd have to go back to Beloit at midday: 'I'm driving my son, John, to Onarga to see a school there. He's at an age where my father thinks he should attend a military academy. So, we're going to the Onarga Military School run by an Army Brigadier, General J.E. Bittinger, who just happens to be a friend of my father. I hope John likes it.

'I've heard about Onarga,' Raj offered. 'It's quite close to my old engineering school at the University of Illinois Urbana-Champaign. Your father is well connected, isn't he?'

'He's a prominent lawyer. I told you he was a top lawyer in New Mexico. And my mother comes from a well-to-do East Coast family. So, yes, we're well connected.' Raj said nothing but couldn't help thinking, *with that family lineage, it will be interesting to see how this all plays out.*

'Will you go to the gurdwara and have langar there on Sunday?' she asked. The Indian words sounded strange coming from her lips, but he was pleased she was trying to learn the correct words and how to use them.

'You know what that date signifies? 13 August?' she added.

He looked at her: her eyes were non-committal and quizzical at the same time. He was desperately trying to remember what meaning that date had. In the end, he shrugged and said, 'You tell me.'

'Sometimes you're just dense, aren't you? One minute you're all romantic and loving and the next you have no idea what I'm talking about.'

Raj said, 'Why don't you put me out of my misery and tell me.'

'Darling, it's our four-month anniversary. Remember we met on 13th April?'

'Of course,' he protested. 'I knew that.'

When Raj walked into the lobby of the Auditorium that Saturday, promptly at noon, he saw the elevator attendant, signalling him over. 'Mrs Lutes asked me to keep an eye out for you,' he said, as Raj entered the elevator.

'Good afternoon. Thanks. Shall we go up?'

'Of course, Sir. Will you and Mrs Lutes be having dinner with us this evening? Do you want me to call Henri and make a reservation?'

'Yes, we'll have dinner, but let Mrs Lutes make the reservation. I'm not sure what time.'

As he got off the elevator, Raj fished in his pocket for a tip.

The elevator attendant, however, while happy to receive the money, said, 'You don't have to do that every time, Sir. Besides, Mrs Lutes takes good care of all of us.'

Raj just gave him a friendly pat on the shoulder and walked over to her apartment.

Louise opened the door immediately but hid behind it. He walked into the room and was blinded by the glare of the sun streaming in through all the windows. Shading his eyes, he turned around, and she was in his arms. She was wearing nothing.

He was always happy when he was with her. And yet, for a while now, he'd been wondering where it all was leading. How long could they keep meeting secretly? Then he would tell himself, *we enjoy one another, so let's just leave it there.* But he knew he wouldn't.

In bed, she stirred against him, snuggling into the crook of his arm. But he could feel her eyes on him. 'What's my man thinking? Does he want more?'

He stroked her back absentmindedly and gave voice to what he'd been thinking. 'Where is this going?'

She raised herself into a sitting position and the sheets fell away from her. Her skin was luminous and golden in the sun's light.

'Oh, but I've got that planned out.'

'Planned out? What do you mean?'

'Listen, darling, whatever it takes, I want to be with you. You're the love of my life, and I won't let you go. Heart and soul, mind, and body, we are One, Raj! Don't you feel that?'

'I do. But how are we going to be together? You have young children. You come from a prominent family. You can't marry me. You'd be stripped of your citizenship if you married an alien who can't become a US citizen. You know the law I'm referring to?'

'Yes, I do. The Cable Act is a horrible law, but I've made plans for all that.'

'Will you abandon your children and parents for me?'

'I'd be the first to admit I'm not a good mother. My children are mostly brought up by *my* mother, who dotes on them. But I can't leave them, at least not yet. In a few years' time, though, I can. And, yes, to answer your question, if I had to, I'd leave them for you. How can you even doubt that?'

'I'd feel guilty if I made you do that,' Raj said.

'Darling, when will you understand that nobody can make me do anything unless I want to? For you, I'd do anything. I'm so lost in you.'

Raj was getting more than a little uncomfortable.

She must have sensed it, because she said, 'I know discussing your emotions isn't easy for you. You told me your whole family is stoic. But, for my sake, let's try to discuss this openly. Can we do that?'

'OK, but first let me make us some tea.'

'My man must have his tea. Can't change his ways,' she said teasingly.

He showered quickly and dressed, then headed for the kitchenette where he made tea from leaves he'd bought a few weeks before in Chicago at the Mumtaz Shop, which sold Indian provisions. He noticed there were more of his foods in the kitchen than hers.

They sat across from one another at the small table. 'Let me tell about my plans,' Louise said. 'But, first, what are the two strings tied on your wrist. Do they have any significance?'

'They do,' Raj said. 'Today is the festival of Rakhi. Do you want to hear about it?'

'Yes, please,' she said leaning forward and taking his wrist in her hands.

'Each year, a sister ties a thread, called a *rakhi*, around her brother's wrist. It symbolizes their love, and blessings for him for a long life. In return, he gives her a token amount of money that signifies he will protect her as long as he lives.'

'What a beautiful sentiment; but why do the sisters need protection? Can't their husbands do that for them?'

'Ah, that's the difference in our societies. When a woman gets married in our society, she technically leaves her family and joins the family of her husband. But what if the husband, or her mother-in-law, mistreats her? Who will protect her?'

'Now I see. The brother guarantees her safety through his protection. How nice. I wish my brother would do that. He's got his own problems, though, with women all over him.'

'Maybe I should get lessons from him,' Raj said playfully.

'Oh no you don't. I'll scratch out the eyes of any woman who comes near you. Can I tell you about my plans now?'

'Of course,' Raj said. He could smell that light floral perfume of hers which permeated the room.

'I call them my three-year plans. We are in 1927, and the plans I've made are for 1928—1930 and then from 1931–1933.'

Raj just nodded.

'First, let me say I won't ever stand in your way. You gave me an understanding of your family life in India and your obligations. You also told me that in April of 1928, you will have been in the US for five years and that one of the promises you made to your mother was that you would return after that. Which would give you enough time to graduate and get some work experience, right? So, with that in mind, I calculated that you'll probably want to leave in the first half of 1928. Am I right?'

When Raj finally said yes, it was an uncomfortable admission that, their passion notwithstanding, he did have other obligations. He was also pained to see that there was a hint of sadness clouding her bright eyes. He didn't have the heart to cause her pain.

Louise sensed his discomfort. She put her hands on his and said, 'Darling, one way or another, one of us is going to endure some pain. And I certainly don't want to be the instrument of that pain.'

He closed his eyes as he held her hands, overwhelmed by her devotion. 'And I don't want to hurt you. It would haunt me forever.'

'Well,' she said, feigning cheerfulness, 'that's why I've thought up these plans. Shall I go on?'

'Sure,' Raj said, but feeling the conversation was not going to end well for either of them.

'Okay: You should leave in 1928 so you can fulfil your family obligations. Go home and get a job in India. Now, didn't you tell me you're temporarily working for Fairbanks Morse in Beloit and that your main employer is Bucyrus Erie in Milwaukee? You asked for specialized training at FM and your employer agreed?'

'Yes,' said Raj. Where was this going, he wondered. And why drag in my employers?

'Well, you see, darling, I can certainly help you there. I like to read and am also a very curious person. I devour books, especially those on philosophy, and, since I met you, on world religions. So once a month or so, I invite professors from Beloit College to my house where we have fierce discussions. You'd be proud of me.'

'I don't know why you're telling me all this,' Raj broke in.

'Do you know Mr W.S. Hovey?'

'The President of Fairbanks Morse?' Raj was incredulous. 'Of course, I know of him. I don't know him personally, though.'

'His wife, Mrs Hovey, is a regular visitor to my recitals as well as to my soirees. So, you see, it may have seemed roundabout, but I was talking about us. Anyway, Mrs Hovey is a friend of mine and I could introduce you to her and put in a good word. She's coming to my concert on the twenty-second. Her husband adores her, and she's is a gracious and lovely woman. There will be no difficulty starting things, and then you can carry on with your own charm, my darling.' Louise paused, and looked at Raj intently. 'Only, you must talk once I put opportunity in your path. You know, beloved, how you sometimes stand silent, when I most want you to make a good impression?'

'I still don't see where this is going.'

'You told me that Bucyrus Erie has a big contract in Sukkur to build a dam on the Indus River and that's close to Quetta where you're from?'

'Yes, and you know my boss, Mr Fykes, has visited Sukkur.'

'Aha,' she exclaimed.

Finally, he allowed himself a faint smile. 'OK, OK, now I get it. I see where you're going. Clever and very devious of you. But I like it.'

'Tell me what you see.'

'If I make a good impression on Mrs Hovey, she might mention me favourably to her husband. And, knowing that I was seconded from Bucyrus and that they have a dam construction project in India, mightn't he just mention that to his Bucyrus counterpart? Before you know it, couldn't the Project Manager at Bucyrus be convinced that a talented, trained engineer, from inside their own company no less, representing them on the ground in Sukkur would be good for them? There's a job for me, then. What a conniving thinker you are, Madam. I love it.'

Raj threw up his hands in wonder and then clapped. He got up, went around to her, put his arms around her and kissed her.

'You know, I'm convinced that with you by my side, there can be no failure. I'll have to set my goals in life even higher. And I'm already an ambitious person.'

There was a delighted smile on Louise's face.

'You'd be guaranteed a well-paying job in India. But, of course, you must win over Mrs Hovey once I introduce her to you. Can you do that?'

'With your help, definitely,' Raj said though he didn't feel quite so convinced inside.

'That is the beginning of my first three-year plan,' Louise declared. 'Let's move on.'

He leaned back in his chair. Things were looking up.

FOURTEEN

Chicago, 13–14 August 1927

'So now that you have a job, or let's hope you have one, you'll go back to India in April of 1928. The first three-year plan begins. And even though we will be separated by continents, we'll be in touch.' Louise's voice was at once determined and hopeful.

'Yes, of course, we can write to each other.'

'Exactly. Look what I've bought for that.'

Louise rushed over to her writing table and took out a box from one of the drawers. 'This is the paper I bought for my letters to you. I'll try to write an exceptionally fine script. The sheets are large and twenty-four to each box. After I have used up six boxes, you must come back. Six boxes of twenty-four papers each will last 144 weeks if I write you once a week, just a few weeks shy of three years. That's long enough to be away from the woman who loves you, and whom you love, wouldn't you say?'

Raj looked at the beige paper, which was legal-sized, slightly thicker than bond and watermarked with faint wavy circles. In the box were twenty-four matching envelopes of thicker stock, where the watermark, also of matching wavy circles, was in a darker print. They were dark enough that anything written on the paper inside the envelope would be hidden from prying eyes.

'Quite distinctive,' he said. 'I'll always know the letter is from you when I see this envelope.'

'I can fold one sheet in half on the long side and write, first, on the folded half, then on the full page inside, and end on the last folded page,' Louise explained. 'Make it like a brochure, like the one I showed you in my studio. That way, if I write in a small script, I can tell you all the news, but also how much I miss you and love you.'

'You do have a fine script. It's slanted way over to the left, and sometimes I can't read it. How do you get that slant?' Raj asked, knowing he was not exactly saying what she wanted to hear.

'When I write, I have the paper almost perpendicular to my body as though I were pushing it away. Then I write with my right hand, the pen tilted towards my body.' She demonstrated as she spoke.

'I see now. The good news is that, if I can't read it too well, no one in my family will be able to either. But I'll keep them locked away in my trunk, so nobody can pry. What will you do with the letters I send you?'

'I'm going to read each letter repeatedly, so it's memorized. I'll keep it on me until I get the next one; then, I'll destroy the older one. You will write, won't you? You have such fine penmanship, and you write so eloquently.'

Raj just nodded. Yes, he liked to write, but mostly about Sikh philosophy. His writing took him deeper into his faith. Sometimes his brother in India complained that the letters he wrote home were so full of his theories on philosophy and '*what are the characteristics of a great person*'; that they offered no real news. He remembered an exceptionally long letter in which he had laid out, with diagrams and specifications, the details of how homes were centrally heated in America.

'Have I lost you already, darling? You seem to disappear in your thoughts. As I was saying, after we exchange letters every two weeks or so for three years, you must come back, darling. Won't you?'

Raj got up and embraced her, holding her body tight against his. 'I will come back,' he said.

He could feel that Louise was getting sad at the thought of their separation, so he tried to cheer her up. 'It's still a long way away. Come on, let's have dinner. Look, the sun is almost set and I'm hungry. Tonight, it's my treat. OK?'

'OK, darling, whatever my man says. Whatever makes him happy, makes me happy.'

At the restaurant, after they had placed their order, she said, 'Would you like to hear the next three-year plan?'

'Your plan from 1931 to 1933? Where am I living? What am I doing? Do I still have the engineering job with Bucyrus Erie in Sukkur?'

Raj was curious, but he was also being careful. He did not want to make promises that he couldn't keep, and he wasn't sure that his vision of his career fit with her dreams of their future.

'Let's take it a step at a time, my impatient one,' she said. 'I want you to plan to get to Chicago on the first of March 1931. I, in turn, will have made my plans so that through that summer I can be in Chicago, four or five days a week. And, we can live together, Raj.'

'That's it? That's a plan for a summer only. What about the rest of the year? Where do you think I'll find a job? Shall I come back and resume my job in the foundry at Bucyrus...after I've spent three years in a mangerial position in Sukkur? What kind of advancement is that?'

As he spoke, Raj knew he was upset, though he couldn't quite put his finger on why. The restaurant, though, was no place to vent his feelings.

Louise was quiet for a moment, and Raj suddenly felt her plans weren't realistic. Rather, she was describing what she wished for.

'But it's only for a short time, darling,' Louise said now. 'We'll have to weather those years any way we can, in the hopes that the next three, and long after that, will be much better. Don't you think a little sacrifice is a small price to pay?'

'And where shall we live after that summer? Will we be together, or will I live alone?' Raj was seething.

'I'll still have my apartment here, though I may have to move into a single room to save money. Since I won't have that many students, I'll have to skimp. I've thought of that, too.'

Raj just nodded. He didn't want to start planning a future with her that already looked bleak to him.

Louise resumed: 'You can also put away a few dollars, say $50 or so a month, from your salary in Sukkur. So, we'll have those savings to fall back on. Then, and I want you to listen carefully to this Raj, I have that Rock River waterfront property that my father bought for me. Remember I showed it to you when we drove out there? Well, I told you that my ex, that wastrel, Shorty, is living there now but we, that is, my parents and I are quite certain that he's using it for trysts. My father has ordered him to vacate that place, and I'm sure he will. Anyway, that property can be sold. I asked a realtor friend of mine, and he said it would sell for $30,000. That could be ours to live on, darling, couldn't it?'

For a moment, Raj was overwhelmed by Louise's determination to find a way for them to be together. 'If our destiny is such, we shall live together,' he said quietly. But he didn't really believe in destiny, only in what one person could carve out for himself.

Louise leant forward and gripped his arm. 'My darling, our destinies are largely in our own hands. You know that. The man who sits down passively and says, "My destiny is willed" never gets anywhere. You are not that kind of a man and I am not that manner of woman. We desire each other with an intense longing. I tell you, we shall have each other! In three years! You promised that you would come back then. Get to Chicago in 1931 and leave the rest to me!'

Once again, Raj was both awed by her resolve and force of character. Before he could say anything though, Frederick and another waiter appeared with their dinners and, as usual, served them with great ceremony.

'When you are living here again, in 1931, you'd have to change a few things, you know.' Louise continued even though she knew she was in uncharted territory.

Raj, with his mouth full of mutton, just looked at her questioningly.

'I would never want you to shave off your beard because I love its softness against me. But the long hair will have to go, darling.'

Raj put down his knife and fork. There was a cold look in his eyes as he said, 'You want me to give up my religion? You know I've told you many times that it's against my religion to cut off my hair.'

'Yes, you have, darling, but I'm only thinking of you, of us. You stand out so much with your beard and turban. Why can't you be like other men? Why don't you want to be anonymous? Can't you do that for me?'

'I see your point. Why not mingle in and be just another Tom, Dick or Harry?'

'Yes, darling, that's it. Nobody would notice us. With your complexion, you could be a southern European.'

Raj had had enough. 'I am not going to change. Not for you and certainly not for anybody else. And I don't want to listen to any of your stupid plans, either. I'm going back in 1928, yes, because I made a promise to my mother and I intend to keep it. I have a family I need to support. I'll save whatever I can from my salary but, if my family needs that $50 a month that you want me to squirrel away, I'll spend it on them. I have a community I need to support. You may not care much for family, but I do. It's in my blood and in my nature.'

With that, Raj dropped his napkin on the table,

pushed back his chair and stood up. 'And now I'm leaving. I need some fresh air.'

He dropped a handful of notes on the table and stalked out. Henri and Frederick came rushing over to Louise's table.

'Madame, is everything all right? There wasn't a problem with the food, I hope.' Henri was solicitous and protective.

'No, Henri, everything is all right. Just a misunderstanding. I'm not hungry either. I think I'll leave as well.'

Under the gaze of curious diners, Louise stood up and made a dignified exit.

Raj was furious.

As he exited the hotel, he turned left and headed uptown, his pace matching his anger. At Jackson Drive, he turned right and went to Lakeshore Drive which fronted the lake. He was walking fast, his mind a whirl. His heavy brogues beat a steady rhythm on the path.

He felt hemmed in by her and pushed at the same time, as though he were being hustled into a corner. Looking up at the tall new buildings being built abutting Grant Park, he felt that, physically, he was also circumscribed, caught between their black silhouettes and the empty blackness of the lake to the right. In a way, he thought, there was a similarity between the tall buildings and the mountain ranges surrounding his beloved hometown of Quetta. But that's where the resemblance ended. For here, everything was ordered and gridded. Planned. Like her plans for them. That's not what he wanted. He longed for the open, disordered rock-strewn pathways of Quetta.

As his legs kept churning up Lakeshore Drive, he remembered how, in Quetta, he would end his dinner on some nights, put on freshly laundered clothes, and hike through the night to his aunt's village miles away. The faint light of the moon lit his way as he would pick his way through the high desert of Baluchistan. He loved those walks—the night breeze fanning him as he walked with forceful purpose, the crunch of pebbles under his thick-soled boots, sometimes the sounds of lizards and snakes slithering away. One night he had stepped on something that moved and he stayed in that position through the night. As daylight came, he saw that his foot was on the head of a snake. He had picked it up, smashed it against a boulder, and continued.

He would usually arrive early in the morning at his relative's house in a small village, quieten their dogs, and fall asleep on a string cot in their courtyard. He would awaken to the crowing of roosters and the mooing from the cows in the sheds. He would walk over to the well, which he had helped dig to a depth of twelve feet, draw a bucket of cold, refreshing water, drink deep and wash himself. Then he would go to the cowshed and, stooping down, drink the cow's warm, fresh milk straight from her udders. His aunt, the one with the broad smile, would come out and greet him and they would sit in the small room set aside to house the Sikh scriptures, the Guru Granth Sahib. His aunt would recite the morning prayers as he sat and listened in a trance-like state. Finished with the morning ritual of 'awakening' the Guru Granth Sahib, she would lead the way to her kitchen. As they talked, she would cook him a hearty peasant breakfast of paranthas made of corn flour. In the centre of the parantha, she would put a large dollop of homemade butter. With this she would serve him freshly made, tangy yogurt, or, sometimes, she would make him a mixture of mustard greens mixed in with spinach. Laced with ginger and other spices, she would add some butter in it, and he would scoop this up with the parantha pieces. On other occasions, she would make him khamiri roti, sourdough bread, and serve it with whatever leftovers there were from the previous night's dinner. He liked it best when she had cold, black lentil daal leftover to serve him.

Slowly, his cousins would drift into the kitchen and then, his uncle. They would all eat from the same platter and drink fresh milk. The companionable chatter would move to the courtyard where they would drink strong tea boiled with sugar and milk in the pot, laced with ginger and cardamom. As one by one his cousins and uncle drifted away from this gathering for their daily chores, his aunt and he would continue to talk as she counselled him on his future. Later, he would hike back.

What delightful memories, he thought, as he walked, ever faster along the darkness that was the lake. There was some urgency, he felt, to rid himself of the memory of her stupid plans.

He had reached the Chicago River and then turned back. As he walked south on Lakeshore Drive towards Burnham Park, his mind was furiously, but logically, considering the plans she had laid out for them. He was torn between his love for her and the duty he felt he had towards his family. Most importantly, he did not want to disappoint his family by cutting his hair and giving up on his religion. He wanted to stay but it would have to be on his terms. He also knew that he had made a commitment to support his family. Why was that so important to him?

'Ghairat.'

That single word came to him and he knew now why he was furious with her. Family came first.

Raj recalled an incident when he was in his late teens. He was already a feared wrestler, trained by his uncle who was the best wrestler in that small town. Raj had a reputation for never backing down and almost always defeated his opponents. Once he had taken his Bull Terrier, Gyp, for a walk when a Pathan with a much larger Alsatian had set his dog on them. Raj had let Gyp loose with a quiet command, 'Attack'. Gyp proceeded to maul the larger dog and the Pathan, after being mercilessly teased about the loss by his friends, had turned up that evening at Raj's home, and challenged him to a fight. Raj had stepped out in front of the house where the Pathan was waiting along with an eager crowd who were expecting to witness a fight. Raj was undaunted. His mind was empty but alert.

Never back down. If you must fight, prepare yourself and attack. Take the fight to your opponent. His uncle's advice, drummed into him, urged him on.

He had, automatically, gone through the wrestler's preparation for a bout: with the palm of his right hand he had struck his left shoulder a hard blow, with the palm of the left, he struck his right shoulder a similar hard blow. Then, with the palm of his right hand, he thwacked his right thigh, and, with his left palm, his left thigh. One-two, one-two. The ritual at once started his blood flowing and it also signalled to his mind that a fight, an attack, was about to begin. He was ready. His opponent and he crouched down and circled each other, looking for an opening to attack.

Looking at his opponent's style, Raj had already mapped out the fight in his head. The Pathan, he noticed, kept his right arm extended. Perhaps to grab him. But, to Raj that was the Pathan's weakness to exploit.

Never back down. Take the fight to them.

Suddenly, Raj lunged forward, grabbed the Pathan's right arm with his left and pulled him towards him. With his opponent off-balance, he caught a handful of his trousers in his right hand and kicked his legs from under him. The Pathan had landed hard on the ground. Then Raj had fallen on him and pinned him down with his shoulders and his hands. The fight was over before it began.

The Pathan had vowed fealty to him and the next day brought a dozen platters of dried fruits and nuts to his house as a token of his friendship. That's the way they did it, Raj mused. Beat them and they're your lifelong friends.

The Pathan had taken him aside and said, 'Brother, you are now a man. You must always act like one.'

Raj had asked, 'What does that mean?'

'*Ghairat,*' the Pathan said. 'Understand the concept of *ghairat* and live by it.'

'What is it?' Raj had asked.

'The one term that defines us and how we look at life. *Ghairat* is a combination of prestige, honour, and a Pathan's ability and willingness to take care of, and defend, if necessary, his territory, his family, his clan, and their belongings. It also encompasses the idea of being truthful and honest, of not breaking your word, of not indulging in bribery, dishonesty, lying, cheating, of not doing anything that would result in shame and loss of face. To be a man of *ghairat,* therefore, you must be strong. You must maintain your prestige.'

'But, what happens if you get beaten, like I beat you?' Raj had enquired.

'You accept the other person's victory, and he will protect you.'

'But I am also told that you Pathans never forget, that you will carry out your revenge even if it takes you generations. You were here to exact revenge for your dog's loss.'

'Yes, you've heard right. My dog's loss was my loss. *Badla.* Revenge also defines us, but only if the other party has resorted to dishonourable ways to cause you or your family, those whom you must protect, harm. Then, yes, *badla,* we will never forgive, nor will we forget. But you, Sardar, have beaten me honourably. There is no shame in that for me.'

So lost was he in his thoughts that Raj did not realize that he had reached Burnham Park. He turned around and made the circuit back to the Chicago River. Finally, after about an hour of brisk walking, he turned around and went back to the grandly lit Buckingham Fountain. Why, he wondered, had he been thinking of that wrestling match and his training?

He looked up at the Auditorium and saw Louise at her window in her apartment, looking out at him. She waved but he didn't have the slightest interest in encouraging her any further. She just didn't understand him, did she? All she cared about was her own pleasure and happiness. Who was she to suggest he cut off his hair? As he thought about her words, his temper bubbled up again. He was walking in circles around the fountain, his hands clenched, muttering his anger at no one. The clock in a nearby tower stuck midnight.

'Hey, you. You Arab. What are you doing here? You think you're Valentino in *The Sheik* with that turban? Why don't you go back home? We don't want you here.'

Raj was instantly focused. He stood still, his mind empty, his wrestler's instincts appraising the situation. There were three men approaching him down one of the paths leading to the fountain.

All of them were big, much bigger than him and they were all well-built. Like college footballers, he thought.

Never back down. Take the fight to them.

His uncle's words came back to him. Now, he understood why he had been thinking of wrestling and his training. There are no coincidences, he thought. My subconscious was thinking that this would happen and was preparing me.

Stepping towards them, he said to one, 'Were you talking to me, you son of a bitch?' His voice was icy in its fury.

'Yeah, you. What are doing here? This is America. Go back to whichever sand pile you came from.'

'OK, big guy, why don't you make me. Which one of you wants it the most?'

The three looked at each other and laughed. 'So, you want to play, do you?' the biggest of the three said.

Raj had assessed the surroundings with his alert eyes. The fountain was behind him, about twenty feet away. The paths leading to the fountain were narrow and had dense flower beds bordering them. They would have to come towards him on the path. There wasn't enough space for them to attack him all at once. They would have to come at him one at a time. This, he knew, was his advantage. He began with the wrestler's preparation, hitting himself with his right and left palms, just as he had been taught. One-two, one-two. He crouched into a wrestler's stance and was ready to fight. He could feel his adrenaline kicking in. At the same time, he was cold and analytically relishing the fight. The fight was mapped out in his mind and over before it began.

The biggest one came at a rush towards Raj. His arms were spread out in front of him, as though he wanted to envelop and crush him. Raj smiled. When the attacker was within ten feet of him, rushing headlong, Raj ran towards him.

Take the fight to them, he remembered.

The attacker hesitated a moment, not expecting a smaller person to rush at him, let alone smile. Raj launched himself at him at a run and kicked him sharply on the shin. His heavy brogues made a solid thwacking sound as it connected with bone. The man howled and began hopping around on his foot. Raj stepped in closer and punched him on his nose. He heard the satisfying sound of the man's nose breaking. Then, as the attacker was staggering back, he used his steel kara and brought it down on the man's cheekbone with a sickening sound. The man cried out in pain and was still unfocussed when Raj pulled him towards himself, ran backwards with him in tow, and then heaved him into the fountain.

The other two men were momentarily taken aback. The second attacker rushed Raj, who still had his back, deliberately, towards the fountain. Nobody could, therefore, attack him from the back. Raj's opponent swung clumsily and wildly, but Raj had stepped aside, to his left. As the man's momentum carried him forward, Raj turned and hit the back of his neck with the edge of his right hand. The man fell forward and hit his head on the fountain's stone edge. Raj bent down and grabbed his ankles and tipped him into the fountain as well.

He turned towards the last of the men. 'Now, do you want to come play with me? This is my sand pile, Brother, come, let me teach you a lesson, too.'

But the man took one look at the two men floundering in the fountain and ran away. Raj walked over to the fountain and glared down at the two men.

'Shall we continue, or have you had enough?'

The two men threw up their hands in surrender and Raj watched them stagger their way over to the far side of the fountain, haul themselves out of it, and lurch off in a pool of water. The biggest one was holding his face in pain.

Raj clapped his hands together and laughed. All his anger drained out of him. The adrenaline that had begun with his anger at Louise and which had escalated with the excitement of the fight, quickly ebbed. He was in a calm, even a euphoric, mood. He was walking over to a bench when he saw Louise running wildly towards him.

'What happened? I saw two or three men and you in fight. Where are they? Are you OK? Did they hurt you?'

Raj was laughing. 'I haven't had so much fun in months. I wish more people in America wanted to fight.'

'You're a fool, Raj. Those men could have beaten you up. There were three of them, all much bigger than you. Didn't you think at all?'

'No, I didn't. They said a few bad things about me, and I taught them a lesson. I'm fine. But look at you. You have next to nothing under your raincoat. Aren't you cold?' With that, he took off his jacket and put it around her shoulders.

'I'm fine now, darling, my man is safe.' She burrowed into his sheltering arms and they walked over to the bench. She sat down at one end of the bench and made Raj lie down with his head on her lap. He did so with a satisfied sigh. She was stroking his beard absent-mindedly with her right hand. The fingers of the left hand seemed to beat out a rhythm on his shoulder.

'Weren't you afraid?'

'No. In fact, if anything, I was excited. I haven't fought in a long time.'

'Where did you learn to brawl like that? You looked like a street fighter.'

Raj looked at her for a long time, not saying anything.

'And that's another thing: Why are you so private? Why can't you let me in? Tell me about yourself, your family, your innermost thoughts? You're like a closed book.'

'Are we having an argument? I thought we just kissed and made up?'

She started laughing, a full-throated sound that was carefree.

'OK. Let's…'

'I learnt to wrestle and build my body in Hoti Mardan. When we get back, I'll show you where it is on the map.'

She was all ears and attuned to him as he spoke of a faraway land, a faraway life but one that he carried with him.

'I learnt some seminal lessons there that shaped me, physically and mentally.'

'How old were you?'

'I was seven. You have to keep interrupting me?'

She made a zipping motion across her lips.

'Next door to our house, in Hoti Mardan, lived my maternal uncle, who was well known as being the best freestyle wrestler in the area. One day, soon after we arrived in Hoti Mardan by train from Quetta…'

'You'll have to tell me about your journeys, won't you?'

He just gave her an exasperated look and continued.

'My uncle took me and my older brother to the open field near the house, or *maidan* as it is called, to play. A group of tough Pathan urchins surrounded us. The Pathans are the native tribe of that area. If you want, I'll explain more about that to you later.'

She just squeezed his hand and nodded. 'Go on with your story.'

'One Pathan teenager challenged my older brother, who was then ten, to a fight. This kind of challenge was all too common in the North-West Frontier Province. It was a test of manliness and your willingness to prove that you could survive. A group of older Pathans gathered and said they would make sure the fight would be a fair one, that is, one-on-one with nobody helping the fighters. This was their code of conduct in action, both in the challenge and the rules by which the challenge would be carried out.

'My brother had been taught a few wrestling tricks by our uncle and proceeded to throw his Pathan opponent to the ground a couple of times. But he was not able to pin him down. He was, nevertheless, declared the winner and the defeated Pathan boy was taunted by one his fellow Pathans that he had been defeated by a Sikh. The boy retorted that '*the Sardars* (the title, meaning 'leader' by which all Sikh men are called, even today) *are Pathans amongst the Hindus.*' That is, they stand out for their physicality and force of personality. Thus, there was no shame attached to being beaten by a Sikh. From that day on, my older brother was treated with respect by all the Pathans.'

'But not me,' he said, 'I was considered too young.'

'And you were, darling. You were seven, you said. Who's exposed to such physical brutality at that age?'

'The Spartans for one...'

But her look of amazed disbelief stopped him. 'What did you do?'

'I was determined to build a stronger body. Who better to ask how to do this than my uncle's mother? I asked her what her son had done to build a powerful body. She told me. At her direction, I began to drink more milk, eat more meat, and down glassfuls of ghee every day.'

'Ghee?'

'Yes, clarified butter. If you boil butter, the dregs are separated and what is left behind is ghee. The best cooking medium.'

'You just drank a glassful of this every day?' Her voice matched the look of disgust on her face. 'Must taste oily and fat. Coagulated.' A shiver ran through her body.

'At first, I didn't like it either but later I looked forward to it. I also started doing exercises. We didn't have any weights or equipment as such, so most of my exercises were body weight exercises consisting of squats, push-ups, chin ups and the like. I used to exercise in the same area as the wrestlers, but being of such a young age, I exercised alone. Later, I began using wooden clubs, shaped like giant bowling pins that weighed 50 lbs each. I would pick up two of these and swing them up and down, in circles, over and around my shoulders, to improve my upper body strength. I walked, ran and hiked up in the surrounding rocky hills to build my lower body strength.'

'Such single-minded focus, such will.' She was looking at him with admiration. 'What happened after all this exercising?'

'By the time I was fourteen, I had developed a large and powerful body. I had acquired a reputation as a skilled wrestler and I regularly beat wrestlers twice my age. I was fearless and fast.'

'What did you look like? Right now, you're skin and bones. I mean, I can feel the muscles beneath, but you've lost a lot of weight, haven't you?'

'You're right. I was about the same size then as I am now, perhaps a little shorter. But my body was all muscles and bigger. I used to dress expensively.'

'In what way?'

'I always wore a silk shirt and I had trousers made of imported Tootal cloth from England. My shoes were expensive leather shoes, also imported from England. Sometimes, I would wear black leather shoes with real gold embroidery, a gift from my wealthy maternal relatives. I tied my turban in a flamboyant way, with one end sticking out of the top of the turban like a coxcomb, like this, and the other end was draped over the shoulder. I wore a colourful Kashmiri woollen shawl.'

'You're making yourself sound like a dandy.'

'But I wasn't. When I walked down the street, everybody moved out of my way or the right to the path was decided there and then.'

'Show off,' she scoffed and gave him a playful punch in the shoulder.

~

'We'll have to find another way, won't we, darling?'

'I'm sure you will,' Raj said. 'Like the Sikh men did in California. Did I ever tell you about Bhagwan Singh and the Sikh-Mexican weddings in California?'

'No, what were they? They sound exotic.'

He could hear a tone of hopeful curiosity in her voice.

'I think I told you that I worked on a peach farm owned by a Sikh immigrant in the summer of 1923 before I joined college at the University of Illinois. Didn't I?'

When Louise shook her head, no, Raj continued.

'Yes, I worked for three months on a farm in the San Joaquin Valley.'

Raj then related to her what Bhagwan Singh had told him of the sham Sikh-Mexican weddings that turned out to be long-lasting marriages.

'That's a strange story. The Mexican women and the Sikh men didn't have a common language or a common culture. How did they make it work?'

Louise was busy scheming, Raj felt.

'Bhagwan Singh told me that they soon found out that the cultural habits and food were not that different from each other. Their children speak Punjabi and Spanish.'

'What religion do they follow? Catholicism? Sikhism?'

'I think neither; but both Bhagwan Singh and Carmen make sure that the children know about morals and what is right and what is wrong.'

'How beautiful. So, there's hope for us, no?'

'There is always hope. I believe God looks after us.'

'Great. Whichever God helps us, I think will be fine.'

'But I don't want to hear any more talk about cutting off my hair. It's a closed subject.'

'I did have a secondary plan…' she began.

He laughed out loud. 'You and your plans.'

'But, seriously darling, I can be the one to change. If you think your family will accept me, I will happily incorporate myself into your family life and be a good and faithful member of your family. Don't you know that?'

He looked up at her, but she was gazing far into the rolling lake in front of them. As though from some void, she said, 'I will come to you as your mistress, if that serves best. What are a few words, uttered perhaps by a man of the mental calibre of priests? Do they mean anything?

Can anything ever be more sacred than our own way of giving ourselves? No. If that seems best, we will gaze deep in each other's eyes, and say "Forever". It will be as true a marriage as any ever achieved by orthodox rites, whether it takes place in Quetta or in Beloit! Whatever is best for you, darling, that must come to pass!'

Raj drew her down to him and they kissed deeply. And then they talked...

Later, the next morning, he was awakened in her apartment by a tune she was humming, a tempestuous air that went up in a crescendo and then crashed down into a soothing, dreamy melody. She kept humming it, as though she was trying to perfect it.

He went over to where she was sitting on one of the armchairs in the living room and asked, 'What is that tune? It sounds new, but it is also familiar.'

'It should be, darling. I'm trying to compose a piece for the piano. I'd like to capture your anger last night and our argument that turned magically into a deeper love, especially those later hours in cool and misty Grant Park, when you lay with your head in my lap. I could have died of happiness! That is what I am trying to get into the music. But such ecstasy cannot be conveyed by my mediums, not in music and not in words.'

'It sounds good to me. I like it. What are you going to title your composition?'

'What I called you last night, "My Greatest King of the Sapphire Night".'

'That's a bit overwrought, don't you think?'

'No, I don't think so. That's how I think of you. That's what I called you. But, if you think it doesn't work then I can call it "One August Night". Is that better?'

'Yes, it is. Now, come here.'

FIFTEEN

Chicago, The Auditorium Hotel, 13 March 1928

'It's your birthday next week, isn't it?' she had asked. 'March 13? Let's have dinner at the Auditorium. It'll be also almost exactly a year ago when we first met on the train. Next week may be the last time I see you for a long while. Will you come, please?'

'Yes, of course I will. Our year has flown by. But why do you say it'll be the last time?'

'You'll be leaving in late March, I know. We'll see if that bond between us holds for three years.'

Not wishing to get into difficult and emotional matters he said, 'I'll see if I can stay longer. I have an interview with GE in Schenectady on 15 March. Mr Fykes made the introduction and I hope I get the job there. If I do, we can see each other from time to time. That would be nice.'

'Ah! There you go, making assumptions. How do you know I'd like that?' She was smiling coyly up at him from lowered eyelids.

He reached up and caressed her cheek lightly with

the back of his hand. She leaned into him. 'I'm not making any assumptions. I'm hoping that you'll ask me to stay on after dinner.'

Her voice, as she sank her face into his chest, was muffled and hoarse, 'You'd have to fight me off if you left.'

~

Raj had gone to Schenectady as planned, but the interview turned out to be a non-event. The manager who interviewed him kept looking at his turban and beard.

'Mr Fykes didn't tell me you were…What are you?'

'I'm a Sikh.'

'And you have to wear that?'

'All the time. Let me make this easy for you. I don't think you have any job here that would interest me.' With that, Raj got up, ready to leave.

'Wait a second. Give me a chance to look at your credentials and let's talk.'

'I feel my credentials are quite good and I'm professionally qualified to work here. At least, that's what Mr Fykes told me. But, honestly, I don't like the way you started off the interview. Are you interested in my ability to work, or how I dress and what religion I am?'

'Of course, I want to know your qualifications. But I also have to make sure that you fit in.'

'Clearly I'm not going to fit in here. Thank you for your time.'

With that curt statement, Raj left and went back to the station to catch the train to New York and from there to Chicago.

In a way, he was relieved. Five years was enough. He needed to get back to his family in Quetta. He knew Louise would be disappointed, but his mind was made up. He was going back.

In her apartment at the Auditorium, on 23 March, the leftovers of dinner were scattered on the small dining table. Instead of going to the restaurant, they had ordered room service since this was going to be their last night together. They had lingered, intimately, over the specialties Henri had sent down from the restaurant upstairs. Neither, though, had had much of an appetite.

'Did you like the roast mutton?' she asked. 'Henri says he never had a client who enjoys it as much as you. Today, he said, he had thrown in some Moroccan spices, so it would taste "Eastern". Did you like it?'

'Yes, I did, very much. Please thank Henri for me. And thank him too for the apple pie he made. I usually like it American-style with a double crust, but I really enjoyed the French apple tart.'

But, even as he said it, his words sounded flat. They matched the flatness in the air between them. A heavy shadow pressed down on both. He was leaving and, try as they might, the sadness could not be escaped. He could see that she was masking her agitation with forced gaiety. Every time she reached out to him, he could feel the slight quiver in her touch, the desperateness with which she grasped his fingers.

'I'm sorry it didn't work out with GE but, I think,

you did the right thing by turning down that horrible-sounding man. What did Fykes say?'

He stood up and went behind her chair. Leaning down he embraced her and kissed her hair. 'It doesn't matter, now, does it? It's going to be all right. We'll go through this together. I will be with you in spirit always.'

She turned sideways and kissed his forearm. 'My strong man. My king! I'll miss you, but, yes, we'll be all right. Just promise to write to me. Every day if you can. Describe your life, your surroundings, tell me how you are settling back in, your family, anything, and everything so I know all about your life away from me.'

'I promise I will.'

Without a word she got up and led him into the bedroom.

~

Much later, both were still awake. Her cheek rested on his shoulder and she was stroking his beard.

'I'm going to miss this softness.'

His left arm was on the curve of her hip. 'I'll miss this softness. I'll miss all of you. I'll miss listening to you playing the piano and explaining harmony to me.'

He slid away from her and left the bed.

'Wait, I have a surprise for you,' he said, as he padded back to the living room and searched in the coat pocket that he had hung there in the closet. He brought out a package and got back in bed with Louise.

'Seeing all that nakedness is making me hungry for you,' she said.

He just put a finger on her lips and said, 'Here, this is for you.'

She looked at the package in her hand and sat down beside him. In the soft light of the bedside table, her skin was glowing. He reached out for her, but she brushed his hand aside.

'Later. What is this?'

'Open it.'

She tore through the packaging to reveal a small wooden box whose lid was fastened with a brass hasp. A fragrant aroma came from the box.

'It smells like roses. What is it?'

Opening the box, Louise saw that there were six vials in the box, each containing a pale-coloured, viscous liquid. She opened a stopper of one of the vials and took a delicate sniff.

'What a heady perfume. What is it and where did you get this?'

'It's attar of roses, made in India. I got it at the Mumtaz Indian store where I buy my tea. Something to remember me by.'

'I'm never going to forget you,' she said dabbing a little of the perfume on her wrist. She rubbed the wrist on his forehead and sniffed deeply.

'My man. I anoint you most unforgettable man, ever.'

They kissed deeply but then, the fact of his impending departure next day overcame her. She slumped back into bed, holding on tightly to him.

'I'm coming with you to New York.'

'It's not necessary. You'll just be sadder and then you must go back to Chicago, alone.'

'I've made up mind. The extra few hours with you are worth it.'

He knew well enough not to argue with her once her mind was made up.

'Then Brooklyn, here we come.'

She settled in, in the crook of his arms, with a deep contented sigh.

'My king.'

Part Three

SIXTEEN

Washington, DC, June 1999

'Are you the person who placed the ad in the *Chicago Tribune* about finding Louise?'

It was June 1999, and the receptionist in my office had told me I had a call from a woman named Leslie, who'd posed this question. I normally didn't take cold calls. But I could feel my spine tingling as though someone had poured ice-cold water down the nape of my neck. I took the call.

'Why are you looking for Louise?' Leslie wanted to know.

The woman was abrupt and to the point.

I told her about the letters I had in my possession, that they were very passionate love letters from Louise to my father. Over the phone line, I felt Leslie lighten up. I could even feel her smiling.

'Your father was the love of her life.'

That stark statement engulfed me. Here, at last, was a person who knew Louise. The long and fitful search I had begun in 1988 was, at long last, over.

'Who are you and how do you know Louise?' I asked.

'I'm married to Louise's grandson. My husband, John, is the son of Louise's son, also named John. A friend of mine, who lives in Chicago, saw your ad, and thought it might be my in-law you were trying to find and called me. I didn't know Granya. But I've heard a lot about her.'

'Granya?' I asked.

'Yes, that's the name Louise was given by her oldest grandchild and everyone called her that. You do know, don't you, that Louise is dead?'

'I thought she might be, but I didn't know for sure. When did she die? Where is she buried?'

'I think she passed in 1963 and, if I'm not mistaken, she's buried in Maryland on one of those islands in the Chesapeake Bay. St Mary's I think.'

I was scribbling away in my awful writing, taking notes on a yellow pad.

'Tell me about her.'

'Well,' she said, 'she was quite a bohemian, very free in her way and not a prude. She was an earthy woman.' 'I tell all my friends about her,' Leslie added, 'she was an example of a strong, independent woman, and my friends and I cherish that type.'

After a few moments of silence during which I absorbed this information, Leslie said, 'You know her daughter Josephine is alive, don't you?'

Of course, I didn't. The news astonished me. I could not have hoped for a better outcome.

'Where does she live, how old is she now, can I meet her, what is her phone number?' All these questions tumbled out of me.

'She lives in Connecticut, and I can give you her number. She's going to be eighty-five in August and plans to celebrate her birthday by going hang-gliding.'

I was overwhelmed with conflicting emotions: Josephine was the one living person who might have a direct knowledge of my father and, perhaps, of his love affair with Louise. I wanted to go further into their story, but I was also aware that if I did so, I would be stepping into unknown territory. I might unearth information I did not want to know, something bad about my father. Something untoward perhaps, some emotional upheaval that had ended the relationship. Something that he had done...

I asked Leslie for Josephine's phone number.

After my call with Leslie, I thought about what my eldest sister had said when I had told her I was writing this book: *What right do you have to investigate this? Why don't you leave it alone? It's his private life—why delve into his secrets?* Instinctively, I dismissed those concerns, as I had earlier.

I picked up the phone and dialled Josephine's number in Connecticut.

When she came on, I had no idea how to proceed; how to tell an eighty-five-year-old woman, whom I did not know, that I was the son of her mother's lover. That I had ardent letters from her to him; that I was trying to learn more. How was I to tell her of my own curiosity and quest?

Josephine had a strong, pleasant, reassuring voice. I began by introducing myself and had just begun to explain why I was calling when she cut me off. I sensed she was as excited as I was.

'I know who you are. You're his son, aren't you?'

And most astounding of all, she said, 'I met your father, Raj, once.'

Apparently, she had been playing outside her house on Chapin Street when he came walking up the pathway to the front door.

'He was tall and handsome. He had a full black beard and wore a turban. I had never met anyone like him, and I was a bit scared. But there was an openness to his face that was striking.'

I wanted to know more, but she said, 'When we meet, I'll give you all the details. Come as soon as you can. I can't wait to meet you: I have so much to tell you about my mother. And I hope you can tell me all about your father.'

By now, both of us had calmed down. I told Josephine of the letters that I'd received from my niece and how, after a long, on-again, off-again search, I had very serendipitously located her. She asked if I could send her the letters, and I said I'd be happy to mail her copies. As we hung up, I realized I had a big smile on my face.

Here, now, was a tangible link between Louise and myself, a person who could tell me what kind of a woman she was and how she lived.

I began to look at my calendar, to plan a visit to Southport. Not only did I have my professional life and financial management consulting business to consider,

I also had to think of my wife and our two young daughters. I needed to make sure that my travels fit in with my wife's active work-travel plans as well.

I called my wife and told her about Josephine. We began a well-rehearsed coordination of calendars: summer was upon us, the girls were out of school, we had summer holiday travel plans, and she was leaving to go to Rabat and then on to Paris, with perhaps a side trip to Frankfurt; meanwhile and I had to go to Cairo and then to Botswana and then to...

A few days later, I called Josephine. 'Josephine,' I began. She cut me short. 'Call me Jo,' she said. I told her I would be able to visit her in August.

'That's fine. I've waited so long, a few more months won't matter.'

She said she had just received the copies of the letters and was going through them avidly. She also asked if she could share them with some friends and with her daughters, Susan and Louise, and her niece and nephew, Jackie and John. I agreed and promised to call her on a regular basis.

'I can't wait to see you,' she said.

Southport, Connecticut, 6 August 1999

Jo and I started calling each other often. As it turned out, she was also a prolific letter writer, just like her mother. Every few weeks, I would get a letter from her typed on her faithful Smith-Corona. The letters were signed

'Jo', with a large free-flowing 'J' and the 'O' turned into a happy face. Apparently, she was a spry eighty-five year old.

On 6 August 1999, I went up to Southport to finally meet her. This was twelve years after I'd found Louise's letters, which pointed to my sporadic, often-thwarted search.

It was about six in the evening when I knocked on her door. And there she was: a petite, handsome woman. She had on a blue, crocheted top adorned with butterflies and a deep pink skirt. Her hair was cut short in a bob. And around her neck was a necklace with a large, enamelled butterfly pendant. She must have a special affinity for butterflies, I thought. Jo had a bright, easy smile, and her eyes crinkled with laugh lines.

She led me inside to a very cosily furnished room, with low, cushioned armchairs. On the walls and on every tabletop were a host of knick-knacks. I later learned she worked at a thrift store in Southport and she couldn't resist buying their curios.

On the walls were four painted plates which Jo identified as various species of anemones. The windflower paintings had been done, Jo told me, by a friend of her mother's as a gift to Louise.

I remembered a reference to similar flowers in one of Louise's letters.

'*Mother tells me that windflowers are blooming on the hills. Did you see windflowers when you were in Wisconsin? I will go into the country and gather some so that I may send you some in your next letter. They are lovely!*'

Jo had a bustling, no-nonsense demeanour. We had just settled in her drawing room when she looked at her watch and suggested we leave for dinner. She had made reservations at an Italian place which had a reputation for getting very crowded.

Over dinner, she asked me about my plans. I was about to begin a long-winded explanation when she touched my arm and said, 'Save the long version for tomorrow, dear; just give me the gist tonight.'

What followed was a brief recounting of my life to date and my ambitions, which included the hope that I could find out more about my father and Louise's time as lovers.

She then told me about her life. She had two daughters but her husband, who had been in the Navy, had died some time ago.

'Guess what I did for my eighty-fifth birthday?' she inquired. I knew, of course, but did not want to rob her of the pleasure of recounting her adventure.

'I went hang-gliding,' she said, and her face turned impish. 'Oh, it was such a thrill! Mind you, I wasn't alone. There was this fellow with me, an instructor, and we were strapped together and harnessed to the same glider. But it was a kick of adrenaline! I knew I'd enjoy it, but I didn't know that it would be so much fun! You should try it, you'd love it.'

Jo liked keeping busy and still worked three jobs. The one that seemed to give her the most pleasure was volunteering at her church's thrift shop, tagging, pricing, and displaying items, then ringing up sales. I kept being amazed at her energy and youthfulness; in that respect, I suspected she took after her mother.

Over dessert and coffee (tea for her), she peppered me with questions. We had agreed that the next day we would start delving into our parents' lives. For the moment, though, she displayed an ingenuous, insatiable curiosity about my work and family.

Suddenly, she reached out and took my right hand. 'Is that the ruby ring my mother gave your father?'

'Yes, it is,' I told her. 'I wear it every day. It reminds me of the mysteries I have to solve.'

'It's a very pretty ring.' There was a catch in her voice. I looked at her and she was teary-eyed and looked very sad.

'Could you take me home, please? I'm tired.'

I dropped her off, and we agreed I would come back around 9:30 the next morning.

~

I arrived at exactly 9:30. Something told me Jo would be a stickler for punctuality. She was ready, but volunteered to give me a short tour of the house before we started. In addition to the drawing room I had seen the day before, there was a formal dining room, a large eat-in kitchen, and an enclosed sun porch where we would sit down to talk.

'Before we begin, let me show you something,' Jo said.

Without waiting for a response, she ran up the stairs. By the time she came down, I had settled myself into one of the wicker chairs in the sunroom, and taken out my Sony recording device.

Jo came down holding something very reverently in her hands. It was a small, rectangular, wooden box, probably seven to eight inches wide, about five inches deep, and four to five inches in height. It was made of a dark wood, probably teak; in the front and the back, top and bottom, were two narrow strips of brass that reinforced the sides, giving it the look of a mysterious treasure chest. In the centre of the box, on the front side, was a diamond-shaped brass plate that housed a lock. The box's handiwork looked familiar, as though it were made in India.

She opened the box, exposing the brass hinges, and I saw that it was lined in reddish-purplish velvet. It looked very plush. Nestled inside the box were six glass vials with ornate stopper tops, each one a different shape. The vials contained a light-coloured, viscous liquid. An exotic perfume spread very quickly in the porch.

She looked up at me and said: 'Do you know what this is?'

I shook my head no.

'These are vials containing attar of roses. You know what attar is, don't you?'

I nodded. Attar is the essential oil of a flower, usually roses.

Later, I looked it up. *Rosa damascena,* the damask rose, is widely grown in India and is used to make attar by a solvent or distillation process. Sixty thousand roses produce just an ounce of essential rose oil. It is very precious and must be diluted with additives because pure rose oil is dangerous if applied directly to the skin. Of course, other flowers are also used to produce essential oils but the best known is the attar of roses.

'This was a present your father gave to my mother. Did you know that? She told me he had bought it in an Indian store in Chicago.'

I was shaking my head, feeling a little numb at this physical manifestation of the link between Raj and Louise. Here was something I was looking at and holding that was held by them. This was history made tangible.

'She treasured this above everything else she had,' Jo was saying. 'I don't know if she ever used it: I know she did not want to see it go.'

As she said this, Jo looked at me sharply and continued: 'You look a little peakish. Shall I make some tea?' I realized I was cold, had goosebumps all over me and my spine was tingling. I nodded a yes.

While she went off to the kitchen, I studied the box and its contents.

The box, while bought in Chicago, had all the bearings of an Indian artisan. It was clearly not machine made, and it wasn't made to very exacting standards. The brass band in the lower right-hand corner of the front of the box, for instance, was just a little bit crooked. It was a gift of love and there was no doubting the preciousness of the contents of the vials. I touched the vials again, and they were cool to the touch. They had been nestled in that box for over seventy years, I realized, since 1927 or 1928, when Louise got it from my father. It had come from a distant land and had been given with love and cherished by her. She had carried it along wherever she went. I wondered how many times she had opened it in his absence and whether it had given her any solace. Or had it become the embodiment of a love unfulfilled and therefore hidden away?

Jo came back then with all the accouterments for tea: a teapot under a cosy, hot milk in a milk jar, a sugar pot, cups and saucers and a small plate of shortbread biscuits. All the china was decorated with small red roses as was the tray. She laughed when she saw the look on my face (was I that transparent?). 'OK. I don't have matching napkins. Shall we begin? Tell me about your father. I want to know about him from your perspective.'

I proceeded to tell her about the father I knew, who was startlingly different from the man her mother had loved.

SEVENTEEN

Southport, Connecticut, 6 August 1999

Jo then explained how my father and her mother had met on a train. 'How do you know that?' I asked.

'Granya told me.'

'Oh, so you also call Louise, Granya. Why is that?'

'Well, all her grandchildren called her that, and it was just easier for me to call her Granya, too, so that the kids knew who I was talking about.'

'Tell me about the train. Why did she tell you?'

'My mother told me everything. She hid nothing from us and was very outgoing and quite unconventional.'

'Yes, that's what Leslie told me.'

Josephine smiled and went on. 'It was the North Shore Line from Milwaukee to Chicago, a very fast train that took just two hours. Did you know the Japanese studied it before they developed the bullet train? It was the first train to have piped music, too.' She then told me about her mother playing solitaire, and my father approaching her by saying, *I can show you a mathematical way of ending that game quickly*. 'Wasn't that a great line?' Jo asked.

Yes, I agreed, a great line. But inside, I was churning. My father said *that*? I could never imagine him being so playful. He was an intellectual, a scholarly type, when I knew him. And who wants to think of one's parent as a sexual being? Not I, I thought, squirming.

But I wanted to keep going. 'What else did she tell you about that meeting?'

'Oh, a great deal. Everything. She invited him to her hotel, and she said she seduced him. You know what else she told me?'

I just shook my head. I was still feeling squeamish thinking about them as lovers.

'She came four times that night!'

'What!' I sputtered, tea spewing out onto my clothes.

There we were, seated on Josephine's porch drinking tea, and she was giving me intimate details about her mother, my father, and a night some seventy years earlier. She said this just as though she was asking me if I wanted another cup of tea, in the same sort of detached, informational tone.

Jo looked at me with benign amusement. 'Oh, come on, now. I'm eighty-five and you're in your fifties: don't tell me this shocks you.'

'Who told you this? You're making this up, aren't you?'

'My mother told me.'

'Your mother told you this? Why would she ever tell you this? Who mentions such details to their child? How old were you?'

'Oh, it was quite some while ago. I told you that she was an incredibly open, unreserved, avant-garde woman, didn't I?'

'Yes, you did.'

'I know I was married at the time we had this conversation. Maybe I was pregnant. She was wistful. I don't know how the subject of your father came up. Maybe I was reminiscing about growing up on Chapin Street in Beloit and told her about playing outside and seeing your father come to our house. I told her I thought he was just a friend, maybe a prospective student.'

Looking for a way to avoid more intimate details, I interrupted and said, 'Wasn't he too old to be a student?'

'Oh, no, she had some students who were professors at Beloit College. Anyway, she told me at that time that he was just a friend. But when we were reminiscing, she confessed that he was the love of her life...and described their first passionate night together. Amazing, isn't it, what she told me. What one remembers?'

Indeed, it is, I thought. A picture of my father came back to me then: he is seated on the veranda of our house with his array of tables and chairs, writing and reading. I was always aware of his mental passions. But the fact that he had lost himself in physical passion was new to me. And I wondered, where had he hidden that physical, passionate side of himself? Why had he partitioned it?

~

'My mother was a planner. It's evident from her letters to him, don't you think?' Jo asked me.

I wasn't doing much thinking. I was just absorbing details from her and learning about a side of my father I didn't know existed.

'Do you remember the plans she made for them? They're in the letters you gave me. She had imagined the two of them living together, possibly in Chicago, after his return from India in 1931. I don't know what was magical about that year, or the time span of three years. Perhaps, she felt my brother and I would be old enough to handle ourselves and that, then, she could break the news to her parents of this overwhelming passion of hers.'

I was nodding. 'And do you think that knowing he would not be able to earn much of a wage on the factory floor, she was planning to acquire some capital for the two of them by selling that River Road property?'

'Yes, I have read that letter.'

But it did make me think about whether my father could ever have accepted such a plan. He was a proud man, a very traditional man. In his mind, it would have been his duty to provide for his family. He would not have wanted to rely on Louise's largesse or her money.

Before I could say anything more, Jo interrupted my train of thought.

EIGHTEEN

Southport, Connecticut, 6 August 1999

'Before we talk of other things, I want to know how you tracked me down. How did you find me?'

'It's been a stop-start search always aided by serendipity,' I said.

'What do you mean?'

'It's been twelve years since I obtained the letters. A niece of mine in Delhi had them.'

'Why and how did she have them?'

'My father gave them to her, she claims.'

'But why her? Didn't he value them?'

'I think he did. That's why he kept them. But I also think that he wanted someone to find out about Louise. To see if she was alive. Perhaps to put a definitive ending to the secret relationship.'

'You think your getting them was a coincidence?'

'No. I don't believe in coincidences. I think he felt I was the one to carry out the search for Louise. That is why he had given me the ring as well so long ago.'

'And yet, if this was his mandate to you, you certainly took your time.'

I gave Jo a cool look: I certainly didn't want her criticism.

'That speaks to my laziness and the fact that the search for Louise, while important, occupied a back-burner for a long time. If it had not been for a couple of lucky breaks and insights, I would not have found you.'

'Tell me all. I'm curious.'

I marshalled my thoughts before telling her of my detective work. At the outset, I explained, I had only her name and address in Beloit. But by chance, I read an article about the US census, which was to take place two years later, in 1990, and about how the government would release the 1920 census in 1992. 'Did you know they wait seventy-two years before releasing the details of any census?'

'I did not know, but how did that help you?' Jo asked.

First, I decided to see if I could find more about her from the census data for 1900 and 1910. I was hoping there were details about her that were not in the letters.

'I was lucky to live near Washington, DC where the National Archives is housed. When I called I was told that all the original census data sheets filled out by enumerators were on microfiche in that one building. The Archives occupies an entire rhomboid-like block between 7th and 8th streets and between Pennsylvania and Constitution Avenues. The architect of the building, John Alexander Pope, wanted to create a temple of history to house the nation's records. He built a structure much like the Parthenon on the Acropolis in Athens.

'After being processed through security, I registered at a desk and was allowed admission to the microfilm room. I made several errors loading and winding the microfilm, but with the help of the very helpful and patient staff, I figured out how the machine worked and called up the census for the year 1910. It took me some time to adjust the speed of the machine and also some more time for me to read the various enumerators' handwriting. I knew Louise was writing letters in the late 1920s, and, while I did not know how old she was when she met my father, I tried to find her details in the census sheets for 1890, 1900, 1910.

'I went back to the Archives in 1992, to view the 1920 census data and see if any additional information could be gleaned. Let me, though, jump to the 1920 census since it contained the latest information on her.'

At this point, I pulled out a ledger-sized photocopy of a 1920 census data sheet and showed it to Jo.

'That's a lot of columns,' she said, 'and I can't read the small type. Can you read them out to me?'

I did so. The enumerator, in the interview with the head of a family, recorded not only the data, but also the time and place it was collected. Each person, at a given address, was listed on the census as was their relation to the head of the household there. Besides the usual details of name and age, the Census also contained the race or colour of the interviewee, the year they were born or immigrated to the US, whether they were citizens, whether they were educated and able to read and write, whether they and their parents were able to speak English, what their mother tongue was if it wasn't English, their trade or occupation, and whether they were employed as a salary or wage earner, or were, themselves, an employer.

I read from the copy. 'Look at this page. The 1920 census was the thirteenth enumeration of America's population. On the 7th day of January, 1920, Catherine J. Richardson, an enumerator for the State of Wisconsin, County of Rock, in Beloit City, in Supervisor's District 1 and in Enumeration District 86, visited 1024 Chapin Street. The visit was to Family 131 and 132: the Roods and the Lutes.'

Jo was leaning forward. Her body was taut. Her lips were pursed.

We were looking at the enumerator's census details on her family, spread across thirty-nine columns. Family 131.

I read out the details. The Rood family was headed by Louise's father, John C. Rood. Born in Wisconsin and aged fifty-nine in 1920; he was a lawyer in general practice and had his own firm. Louise's mother, Jennie (Merrill), also born in Wisconsin and listed as being fifty-eight years of age, had 'None' listed as her occupation. Louise's grandparents are listed as being born in New York.

John Rood's mother, Louise's grandmother, Susan C. Rood, also lived with them and is enumerated with them.

'I know most of this information, but I did not know about my maternal grandparents being born in New York.'

In addition to Louise's parents, there was a second family, listed and enumerated at the same address.

'Look at this detail,' I told her. 'It surprised me when I first saw it.'

I read out the specifics. Listed as Family 132, and living at the same address as the Roods, was a family headed by Frank E. Lutes, a Canadian then aged thirty-six. He had immigrated to the US in 1900 and become a naturalized citizen in 1903. He was employed as a wage-earning 'Adjuster' for the Water, Gas and Electric Company of Beloit. His wife was listed as Louise R. (for Rood, I suppose) Lutes, born in Wisconsin and aged thirty-one at this time.

Louise was listed as a self-employed music teacher. Listed under Frank and Louise were their two children, living with them. John R. was nine in 1920 and his sister, Josephine L., is listed as being five.

'There you are, Jo. You were five when this was taken. And, if my father was seeing your mother in 1927, you were twelve then, right?'

'That sounds right.'

'But there were some things that surprised me. I was not prepared for those details.'

'What were they?' Jo enquired.

'First, your father was still living at that address. What happened to him?'

'I guess he was living there at the time of the census. I do know that my mother divorced my father for his philandering ways and for his inability to bring in sufficient income to sustain our family. Her parents helped them out, but my sense is that my grandparents did not think highly of my father.'

'After the divorce, didn't he live elsewhere?'

'I think so, but only for a time. My mother found out that he was having an affair with a woman of ill-repute. So, she brought him back to live with her, despite her parents' protests. But it didn't last long, and he moved out to a property she owned on River Road, on the road to Janesville.'

'I take it he wasn't living there when your mother began a relationship with my father?'

'No, he wasn't.'

'What else surprised you?'

'Just that, according to the census, Louise was older than my father. Her census-listed age would put her year of birth as 1889. This would make Louise some ten years older than my father, who was born in 1899.'

'I can't comment on that. Love has no boundaries?'

'I grant you that. Finally, you and John lived at Chapin Street with her. Where were you in 1928, when she was writing these letters? Where were you in 1927, when she and my father began their love affair? How did they hide their relationship from her parents and from you if all of you lived in the same house? Weren't they meeting in Beloit?'

'They certainly met once in Beloit. Raj came to the studio at 1024 Chapin. The many other times they met, she told me, was at her apartment at the Auditorium Hotel. Granya also told me that she met him once in South Milwaukee where he had a room in a house. That was awkward, so she never went back there.'

'I do remember reading my father's letter to his family in India that he always tried to get a room in a house owned by older people.'

'Why older people?' Jo asked.

'I think he wrote that older people always kept their house nicely, and sometimes overly heated. His heating bill was, therefore, reduced considerably.'

'Was he poor?'

'I learned an interesting fact about my father. Even when he had little money, he behaved as though he were a rich person. He spent without thinking about the future. Mind you, he didn't spend on frivolous things, but on food, books, essentials; he was a spendthrift. Growing up, we were comfortably middle-class, but our lifestyle was one of privilege and wealth.'

'What was he thinking, spending like that? Didn't he plan for the future?' Jo was appropriately aghast.

'Yes, he did. His plan for the future consisted of a deep and utter faith that God would provide him with money, whenever he wanted it.'

'Did the census data give you any breakthrough information?'

'Not really. I had more details, but I was no closer to finding out if she was alive and, if so, where she lived.'

'What did you do next?'

NINETEEN

Southport, Connecticut, 6 August 1999

'I had another serendipitous moment.'

Jo was dismissive of that thought. 'I'm not sure it's all chance the way you make it out to be. Even though you were not active in the search, your mind was probably engaged in resolving the questions you had. Your subconscious continued to prompt you with ideas.'

'A few days after my visit to the National Archives, I felt an urge to go to a Sikh gurdwara. Now that I had more knowledge about Louise, I could plan next steps. But what should those be? I was at a dead-end. I needed to think, and I thought the gurdwara would be the place to do it.'

'Is that a temple? Interesting that you went to a temple to think.'

I explained that gurdwara is a combination of the well-known word guru, or teacher, and *dwara*, or doorway. Hence, gurdwara literally means the doorway to the guru. I had a need to sit quietly, amidst the familiar hubbub of a Sikh service. 'The gurdwara is a place where congregants collect, usually on Sundays, to pray together. When I go there, I get lost in the familiar womb-like sounds and the rhythms of the service. Often, I find myself in a sort of trance.'

'A trance? That sounds mystical.'

'I didn't mean for it to come out that way. Just that I feel like I'm in a free state, able to fly in any direction. My mind wanders.'

'All this in a temple? What does it look like, your gurdwara, and how do you conduct prayers and services?'

'I'm not an orthodox Sikh so I'll tell you how I visit a gurdwara. By the way, my father was the least orthodox Sikh and the most devout Sikh I've known.'

'How come?'

'When I knew him, he was already in his fifties. He never went to a gurdwara. He did not believe in rituals. Yet, in his heart, and especially in his mind, he was an admirer of the tenets and the philosophy of Sikhism. He examined these closely, almost in an obsessive manner, and wrote widely about them. He was almost asocial, in that he did not want to exchange small talk with anyone. But get him on any topic of Sikhism, and he directly engaged you. He was animated and passionate; you almost wondered how you could get him to *stop* talking about it.'

'I think I understand what you're saying. Do you think your father being a Sikh is central to the story?'

'Yes,' I said, without hesitation.

'Then, tell me, briefly, what I should know about your religion. I've never spoken to a Sikh before.'

I looked at her for a long moment, taking time to collect my thoughts.

I told Jo that in our religion there is no intermediary between God and one's self—so no priests. The journey to God is personal and internal, and outside help is of no use. Sikhism is a monotheistic religion. God is omnipresent, and he was not brought into this world. In fact, we believe He existed before time and this world. He exists now, and He will continue to exist when everything else ceases to be. That is why He is the essential Truth, and our physical journey is meant to be used to find our way back to Him.

'The community runs the gurdwara, using donations from the congregants, and granthis, people who study our scriptures, or granth, sing hymns from it.'

I went on to explain the basic tenets of Sikhism: that everyone is equal regardless of gender, race, and also, more importantly in the context of India, of caste.

'Why is that important?' Jo wanted to know.

'You are born into a caste and consigned to it for life,' I answered. 'You cannot work your way out of it. After the service at a gurdwara, lunch is served in the food hall. Everyone sits on the floor, together, and eats food prepared by the congregants in the same kitchen. A high-caste Hindu would never do that. He wouldn't sit with a low-caste person, and he would never eat food prepared by a low-caste person.'

'So, this is equality in practice? And Sikhs are not Hindus?'

'Yes, to equality. No, we are not Hindus. We have our own separate and distinct religion. Our faith has three basic tenets: make an honest living, share your wealth, and meditate on Him.'

'What about the hair?'

'...the turban? It's usually the first question I get asked by non-Sikhs. I'm surprised you waited so long. Sikhism was started by a teacher, a Guru, who was then followed by nine others, each appointed by his predecessor. The rise of Sikhism paralleled the rise of the Mughal empire in India, in the late fifteenth century and into the sixteenth and seventeenth.'

'One of the Mughal kings built the Taj Mahal, didn't he?'

'That's right. The Mughals were Muslims who were descendants of Turks and the Mongols. Many were visionary; some were narrow in their bigotry. The last important Mughal was especially alarmed by the rise of Sikhism in the Punjab and sought to defuse its popularity by eradicating us. Prior to this, Sikhs were indistinguishable from the rest of the population in northern India: in truth, we Sikhs are the same, ethnically, as the Hindus and the Muslims in the Punjab. We all look alike.'

'And long hair was meant to set you apart?'

'It was the tenth Guru's vision: to physically identify you as a Sikh so you could not hide. You could not deny your faith. It was a way to build solidarity and a method to force one to defend oneself.'

'That seems strange and perverse to me.'

'Maybe so, but it succeeded.'

'That's one reason. There are others, too. For instance, the turban simply is a way to keep the hair tidy. It became and remains the conspicuous symbol of a Sikh.'

'But other people wear turbans, too. Arabs...'

'They do but theirs is a different shape and not a constant headwear. Ours is.'

In the gurdwara, listening to the kirtan, I felt myself slipping, unconsciously, into the world of familiarity, as if I had returned to childhood, listening to my mother's kirtan at home. There, she would sing the daily prayers, and her bell-like voice—from the room set aside for this function, up on the mezzanine—would be like a soothing balm that descended on all of us throughout the house. There were many times when I would see my father, at his desk writing or reading, and he would have stopped, his head would be cocked towards her sound and the hymn.

It was through this lens of the familiar that I began to hear the words of the hymn being sung by the raagis and focused on them.

'Ram simar man, pachtayenga…'

'Dwell on His Name, O Mind,
Not on greed, nor on wealth,
Not even in your youthful strength
All these will crumble to dust
And, too soon, you will realize
That you have no time left,
Listen, Kabir says, in the company
Of Good Men is your salvation.'

Simmer is an interesting word. In cooking, it means keeping the liquid just below the boiling point. In Punjabi, a similar word, *simar,* means to let one's thoughts hover over or dwell on a point. Keeping at it, at a certain tension, but not letting it boil over or overflow. And, out of that dwelling may come insight. Exactly what I was hearing in the first hymn: '*Ram simar man...*' Dwell on His name, O Mind.

I listened to the rest of the kirtan, more focused on the words. My mind, however, was simmering with subconscious thoughts as to where next I could get traction in my search for Louise.

My mind roamed over to one of my many visits to Gaborone, Botswana, where I had an office. I had no idea why I was thinking of that, but I was. As I do in all cities where I visit, I was looking in the telephone directory there to see if there were any Sikh names. This was easy enough because all Sikh men have Singh as their last, or as their middle, name. Singh, the Sikh word for lion. And all Sikh women, similarly, are Kaur, or princess.

I found several Singhs in the Gaborone directory and called one at random. Sure enough, he was a Sikh, and he invited me to the local gurdwara for the service.

I went the next day, which happened to be a Sunday, and was humbled by the hospitality and the fervour with which I, a visiting Sikh, was made to feel at home. Over a prolonged visit to my host's house after the service, he asked about my name and informed me that it was a very unusual family name for a Sikh and that he had not come across any in his hobby as a genealogist.

And, suddenly, right there, in the gurdwara in Sterling, Virginia, thinking of that conversation in Gaborone, my mind stopped simmering and presented me with the next step.

'You had to hire a genealogist?'

'Yes. And a serendipitous hymn, *Ram simar man,* took me there.'

~

And so, I shifted my focus to Beloit, Wisconsin, where Louise was listed in the 1920 census. I looked up the number of the town hall there and started making some calls. The town hall did not have any pertinent records and pointed me to the municipal court. They were not much help either and suggested I try the library.

I didn't find anything new there either. However, the librarian did give me the names of two historical societies which she thought could help. When I asked about genealogists, she said they had a number of professionals who regularly helped people trace family members. She gave me the details of three.

I did not hold out much hope, but I called the first person on the list. My call was answered by a woman, Elsie E. Davis, who told me in a very professional, no-nonsense voice, about the services she would perform: from looking at the Index of Births through 1905, to the Registration of Marriages and Death Records, as well as Social Security records to see if Louise was still alive.

She would do these tasks, and anything else she thought was necessary, then write up a report on her findings and submit it to me with all pertinent documents attached.

How much is this going to cost? I had asked cautiously. She felt it would take only a day or so to complete the work. Her fee was a mere $5 per hour, and she estimated a total outlay of about $40 plus any incidental costs. I was astounded and agreed readily.

Her report came a few weeks later. All the papers had been very professionally squared up and stapled neatly. Attached was a final bill of $30.75. But beyond an odd fact or two, there wasn't much. 'However, I did learn that you were born on 4 August 1914,' I told Jo.

'But you knew that from the census report, right?'

'…but, like your brother, John, you also had a delayed birth certificate that was registered, almost twenty years later, on 1 December 1934.'

'Oh. I wonder why?'

'I also learned more about Louise's divorce. She filed a suit in December 1922 and obtained a decree in 1923. The genealogist added, "However, the 1925 thru 1930 Beloit City Directories shows this couple again residing at the address, 1024 Chapin Street. No remarriage found in Rock County." This was also, as you know, what we saw in the Census.'

Jo nodded and said, 'Because if my father was living with us, how safe was it for your father to visit, is that what you mean?'

When I nodded, she said, 'But I think, as I told you earlier, he had moved out to the River Road lodge in 1925 or 1926. I remember my mother driving me there and sending me into the lodge to check on my father, and, sure enough, he was there at the lodge with a couple of his friends and a few women. He was sheepish but not apologetic. In fact, he was mad that Louise had taken me there to spy on him. So, I went running back to the car and we left.'

Beyond this, the genealogist, despite my hopes, had found nothing else. Once again, I was lost.

TWENTY

Southport, Connecticut, 6 August 1999

'When you were "lost", as you put it, what did you do? Were you actively thinking of new ways to locate my mother?'

'Not really. I used to get upset.'

'Upset? But why?'

'Some time ago, I found a trait in myself that I really didn't care for, but which I utilized from time to time: I had to get angry at something, even myself, to get motivated.'

'Why didn't you just hire a private investigator? That would have taken out all the angst and put you in the hands of a professional who probably had more tools than you.'

'You know, Jo, I never believed that it was an option. I did think of it, but, quite honestly, I wanted to solve this mystery myself.'

'Why?'

'My father gave me the ring. I felt it was his way of urging me on a pursuit.'

'So, what else did you do?'

'There was another search that beckoned, one that I was reluctant to tackle.'

'For your father?'

I looked at Jo with a start.

I nodded.

Whenever I was at a dead-end, I told Jo, I re-read Louise's letters. Her motivations and sentiments were clear enough. His were not since I had only one side of the conversation. However, in listening to her side, I could also decipher, between the lines, some of what he must have been saying.

I believe that nothing happens in isolation, and nothing happens in a vacuum. There are no such things as coincidences. If, therefore, my father gave me the ring, what imperative was he passing on to me? You can enjoy this for what it is, he seemed to have implied, or you can decipher the story behind it. If you find out what it was, and what it represented to me, go ahead. So, despite my discomfiture, I continued.

'I remember your father when he was quite young. What did he look like when he was older?'

I pulled out several photographs from my briefcase, including one, taken in 1902 in a studio in Quetta. 'This is my grandfather, Gopal Singh, with his three oldest sons.

By the way, he went on to have six more children with his wife. At the time the picture was made, the eldest son, Dildar Singh was six, my father was three—that's him on the right, and the newly born third son is Shiv Charan Singh.'

'What a priceless picture. But your grandfather doesn't quite look Sikh, let alone someone from India. He looks like Genghis Khan.'

'You're right in a way. He's got high cheekbones, and with his wispy beard, he almost looks as though he had some of Genghis Khan's Mongolian blood in him.'

We looked at the image together. My grandfather sits on a wooden armchair, the baby on his lap and his two older boys on either side, Dildar Singh on his right, my father to his left. Behind them is a striped printed backdrop of the sort often seen in formal studio images of a certain era. The sepia-toned image was made by the studio of C. Sorabji of Bruce Road in Quetta and the studio's insignia is at the bottom of the image.

My grandfather has on a knee-length long coat of some light colour, and tight-fitting trousers that are also light. His turban, also of a light colour, is unusually untidy and very large. He is looking directly at the camera. He is not smiling.

My father and his older brother are dressed alike: both have on knee-length, buttoned-up coats, with flaps covering the buttons. A tiny belt cinches the coat across the waist. My father's gaze is almost challenging, as though he is daring the world, through the photographer, to say something to him. The stances of the two brothers are indicative of their personalities: the elder has an open curiosity, while my father has a swagger, with his left hand in his coat pocket, head cocked to the right, right hand resting idly on the armchair. He has on an embroidered Afghan-type hat. On his feet are gold-embroidered shoes with a curling tip, typical of that region.

At three, my father was already different from his brother: he has a more mature personality and seems to have a bedrock of self-esteem. His eyes are not different from later pictures of him as an adult. They are eyes that don't blink, that look at you with aloofness and indifference. But the eyes also hint at an underlying resoluteness and a deep well of confidence. The eyes send a clear message: don't get in my way.

'His eyes are reserved,' said Jo. 'But clearly, my mother saw something else in those eyes that invited her in.'

I then showed Jo an image of my family from 1954 and identified everybody.

I vividly remember the day that picture was shot. My oldest sister had just been engaged. Her in-laws-to-be wanted a formal picture of our family, and Mr Sathe, of Sathe Photo Studio in Bistupur Market, Jamshedpur, was called to our house.

He came with an enormous field camera that was mounted on a tripod, and which produced very sharp images. It was that old-fashioned type where the photographer went under a cloth hood and then, once the image was composed and focused, used a mechanical cable release to set off the shutter. The images on the plate that the photographer sees are reversed, vertically and horizontally, and framing the subjects is an art. He produced a superb black and white image.

'How old are you there?'

'I was probably ten and had been playing with my brother in our garden, the usual rough and tumble games, although our mother kept telling us not to get our formal clothes all dirty and rumpled before the photo was taken. But we ignored her. Both of us were wearing grey flannel trousers and dark coloured (maroon, I seem to remember), long-sleeved shirts. Our mother, an experienced seamstress, had made our trousers and shirts. Both of us were also wearing maroon turbans. My sisters were wearing their best outfits. My mother was decked out in a black sari with large roses in faded shades of light cream with a touch of red. She has one end of the sari draped around her neck like a scarf. My father was in a dark suit, a white shirt, and a patterned tie. He had crossed his knees, and you can see the Argyle-patterned woollen socks he had on under his shiny brown brogues. Those woollen socks were always knitted for him by my mother, who made him three or four pairs every year. They were always woollen, always patterned in a hound's tooth design, sometimes in a bird's eye, sometimes in a cable stitch, and he wore them winter and summer because, he said, they kept his feet warm in the winter and cool in the summer. Look at his right hand: it's clenched in a fist. He always did that in photographs. I think he was uncomfortable in those situations.'

All of us, in that formal image, are looking directly at the camera with unflinching gazes, and as admonished by Mr Sathe, we have no smiles on our faces. We are not grim: just formal. My parents and eldest sister are sitting on armchairs—the same 'victim's chairs' that were usually on the veranda. The rest of us are standing: my two older sisters on the left and right, my younger brother in the middle next to me. We have all been arranged by Mr Sathe at one end of our garden. In the background, you can see my mother's beloved flowering shrubs, many planted in flower beds, but quite a few planted in terracotta pots that ringed the flower beds.

Our maali was charged with watering all of them every day. And, every day, he would report one or two of the terracotta pots broken or chipped by cricket balls, or hockey balls, by catapult shots as my brother and our friends and I played pick-up cricket or field hockey or just chased each other in that garden. My mother would sternly tell us to go and play in the stadium near our house or in the *maidan*, an open field, next to the stadium. We would do so for a day or so but then revert to our garden.

'Why is your belt slanted on your waist?' Jo the sharp observer asked me.

'I remember that we were playing cowboys and Indians that day.'

'Why on earth would you be playing that in India?'

'I told you, I was educated at a Jesuit school. The Fathers showed us Westerns most Saturdays. After the Saturday morning drill…'

'A drill? What was that?'

'The entire school formed into companies and marched up and down Loyola's playing fields while

John Phillip Souza's marching music blared out from loudspeakers.'

'Which company were you in?'

'I don't recall, but the day I entered high school, that is, the sixth standard, I was named the head of a company. Just as I was named patrol leader of the Panther patrol in the Boy Scouts.'

'A natural leader?'

'No, I had a beard that was about to sprout and, perhaps, looked older because of the turban.'

'How old were you then?'

'About eleven.'

'OK so when movies...'

'Yes, it was movie time on Saturday mornings. Unless you had done something that warranted you to report for jug, a sort of punishment. In this case, you had to sit in your classroom and copy the log tables. The movies were shown to the entire school in the school's auditorium. If they weren't Westerns, they were stories of knights in shining armour, or of pirates glugging rum sitting on casks, or of Second World War battles. Then there would be the odd romance, but I think the priests mostly kept us away from that genre.'

'Did you have a favourite Western hero?'

'Oddly enough, I did. Randolph Scott.'

'When you played that game, who were the Indians and who were the cowboys?'

'Naturally, I was a cowboy—the laconic hero type. The Indians were played by those in our crowd at the fringes.'

'How do you feel about that?'

'At that time, I didn't give it a thought. I wanted to be a winner. But now, I see that there were no winners.'

'What a handsome family. Your mother was very pretty. And look at your father. He's aged into a very distinguished looking person. His eyes remain arresting. How old is he here?'

'My mother is forty, my father fifty-five.'

'You look like a real mix—your mouth and lips and the shape of your face are those of your mother, but your nose, your forehead and your eyes are those of your father. You have your mother's softness. Do you have a copy of this on display at home?'

'I don't but I had copies of it with me in Oman on one of my business trips to the Sultanate in 1975. On an earlier trip, I had met an Indian artist in the souk in Muscat. I had admired his pen and ink drawings and portraits. I asked him to make sketches from these photographs, but only of my parents, and he did so. He has superbly captured my parents' features and expressions. Those drawings are hanging over my desk in the den.'

'Looking down on you as you are at the desk?'

'Yes.'

As I look up now, both are looking at me directly. I wonder as I type this, what, if anything, they are thinking.

My father was always supportive of my endeavours. I wonder if he is unhappy that I am attempting to discover his secrets. His gaze doesn't tell me anything.

For my siblings and me, my father was a reserved, detached figure.

My earliest memory of him is from when he was already in his fifties. His hair and beard had turned salt-and-pepper. He was married with five children, in a senior management position in the largest steel plant in India. That father had a formidable mind and physique and was passionately engrossed in studying and writing about Sikh religious philosophy. He was a man of fixed habits, of distant ways, of authority.

In my mind, he was a scholar, someone whose lofty ideas and philosophical theories I did not understand. His search for the essence of his religion, a religion I shared with him, did not at all capture my heart as it did his. I could see that he had willingly waded into a sea of ideas and ideals. I stood on the shore watching him. At every 'eureka' moment he would burst into my space and declaim his new understanding. I simply nodded hoping that I could revert to my book, my homework, my idleness.

This identity, as a deep thinker in an ivory tower, was abetted by my mother who kept him in a bubble of sorts. By this I mean that she created an inviolable space around him that we children were not able, or allowed, to invade easily. In that space he read, he wrote, he developed his theses on the philosophy of the Sikh religion.

By the time my father returned from work, it would

be about five-thirty in the evening. We would all have tea out on the veranda. While we talked, he would be quiet. He would nod and perhaps make a brief comment, but otherwise, he was immersed in his thoughts. Dusk, and soon darkness, would take over. The chirping of birds, the mesmerizing chittering of cicadas, would have ended. Playtime was over. There were no outings after dark. Up until 9 p.m., which was our usual dinner time, we were meant to do our homework and any other tasks that were school related. Most of us finished these quite quickly, so that we were free to do anything after about 7 p.m.

Meanwhile, he pursued his reading and writing with his setup of tables and chairs.

We could do anything but create a hullabaloo. In the small configuration of our house, the veranda was forbidden territory. It was marked out for and by him. Mr Pinto, his typist, would be ensconced in the adjoining drawing room with his clickety-clacking typewriter. We could not go there either, lest we disturb him. This left the dining room, the very large, dimly lit, step-down open courtyard, the bedroom, and the kitchen.

The veranda was off limits to us for two reasons: first, our mother forbade us to go there because we would disturb our father in his writing; second, and more important to us, if we ventured there, there was a clear likelihood that we would end up in the 'victim's chair' discussing philosophy with him.

Truth be told, we children were all afraid of him. Not only had my mother created an island for him to work in, but she had also made him into something of a bogeyman: 'Wait till your father comes home, and I'll tell him what you did.' He was made into the dispenser of punishment—a slap, a smart rap on your outstretched hands with a hockey stick, or, if you were, lucky, just a cold stare. His detachment was not just self-imposed; it was also accentuated by us who gave him a wide berth.

While those physical boundaries were onerous, more demanding was the fact that we could not raise the noise level to the point where it intruded on my father's consciousness. My brother and I, therefore, were not running around playing hide and seek, for instance. Nor were we engaged in wrestling each other, another favourite pastime if we were not horsing around. On the odd occasion when we did fight, the physical tugging, pushing, or boxing would all be done silently. As furious as we might have been at each other, for whatever peccadillos or slights we may have imagined, both of us feared the wrath of our father. In suppressed grunts of pain, we battled on. My brother usually bested me.

In keeping with the requirement for near silence, we did not have a TV or radio, so any entertainment would have to be self-generated and, above all, quiet. We played cards, quietly, for instance. We were encouraged to read. Or we went into the kitchen and talked to our mother as she, and the cook, prepared dinner. For me, that was the ideal place: I could see my mother skilfully preparing dinner, and I could ask her questions about recipes, or get samples of what she was making for that evening.

In writing this now, I can see that the measures imposed on us sound draconian and stifling. They were not. We seemed to enjoy the quiet time, and I used to get in a lot of reading, if not indolence, in my constant state of inertia. In this respect, it turns out, that, like my father, I also liked my quiet time. To this day, no matter how late I return home at night, and no matter how tired I am, I need to sit down and decompress alone for some time.

~

This imposed distance, between my father and me, was further enforced by my lack of curiosity, at that time, about him, and his habit of never speaking about himself. I never asked, and he never told. He spoke of his siblings and his belief in keeping strong family ties. I remember him saying that our individual fates, as children, were tied to the fate of the entire family; that is, if one of us fell, all of us were diminished by that degree. Beyond that, he was silent and absorbed in his books.

I hardly spent any time with my father when I became an adult. When I left high school, just shy of my sixteenth birthday, I went to a college in Chandigarh, about 800 miles away, north from my hometown of Jamshedpur. My father, who had retired earlier that year, got a consulting job in a friend's engineering firm in a smaller town about eighty miles from Jamshedpur. He would spend the week at work and return home for weekends. I returned to Jamshedpur from Chandigarh after the university exams, but also because I was expelled from the college for unruly behaviour. Soon after I came back, my father was retained by the Government of the Punjab as a special technical advisor to help them establish heavy industries in that state. By coincidence, he was to be based in Chandigarh. We simply exchanged cities.

I saw him and my mother in Chandigarh briefly, for two weeks or so, as I was preparing to go to England for accountancy studies in February 1966. From 1966 until 1974, when he passed away, I saw my parents on two occasions, in 1970 and 1974, for two weeks each time.

Distance, both geographical and mental, kept us apart.

How, then, to find out more about a father whom I never asked about himself and who also never shared?

The letters from Louise to my father that I had read and re-read told of a passionate man.

I did not and could not know the man who, in his twenties and single, had so captivated the heart and mind of this woman with his physical passion and charm. I could not even imagine him with those traits. I could not see him as a handsome, young man. I could only see the passionate scholar.

It is quite possible, as I now rationalize, that he could have been both persons: the man of passion, in his youth, provoking love from Louise, as well as the aloof and taciturn father I knew.

I decided I needed to find out more about him.

There was a vague memory tugging at my subconscious, something important which, when I first saw it, I wanted to dive into. But then other, more urgent matters diverted my attention.

I remembered what it was.

TWENTY-ONE

Southport, Connecticut, 6 August 1999

My father had given me a folder during my visit to Jamshedpur in January, 1974. The last time I had consulted the folder was in the mid-1980s when I was editing his manuscript on *Japji*, the long meditative prayer found at the beginning of the Guru Granth Sahib. I had stored the folder after that. I remembered, though, that it contained some personal information about his life. Perhaps, I thought, there might be a mention of Louise in that folder.

I located the Bankers Boxes in the basement storage area of our house, in which I kept his files and manuscripts in my possession. There, among everything else, I found the folder.

I also found the folder that contained all his letters from America to his family in India. Mr Pinto had typed them up for my father. While they spanned the entire length of his stay in America, from 1923 to 1928, there were very few letters in the 1927 and 1928 sections—that is, in the years that he knew Louise.

'Like father, like son. Do you see how much of him has rubbed off on you? Mr Pinto typed them up for Raj. By the way, do you ever refer to him as Raj or Rajinder?' Jo asked.

'Neither. Calling your parent by their given names is not done in our society. We are taught to address our elders by the relationship they have to us. To your other point, maybe I'm like my father, but I haven't made it a point to be like him, nor am I consciously copying him.'

I did not want to talk about myself to Jo. In that regard, I *was* being like my father.

I proceeded to tell her about the folder. During my last visit with my parents in Jamshedpur in January 1974, before their deaths in September of that year, I went up to the large sunroom and porch where my father liked to work in their new house. From the porch and his work area, he could see my mother in the kitchen, or in the drawing room chatting with her friends, and he could also see the front gate. He had constructed that house just so: From his vantage point, he could see almost every part of the house except for the bedrooms. He liked space, and this construct allowed him an unfettered view of a large portion of the house and the exterior.

By now he had advanced cataracts. His work set-up of three surrounding tables had not changed much from earlier times, but on the table on the left, he now had a goose-necked lamp with a high wattage bulb that hovered perilously low and shone a very bright light over his work. Also, on that table was a powerful magnifying glass. He would shine the light on what he was reading and look through the magnifying glass to enlarge the print. I was afraid that using this system, he might generate enough heat to set fire to his papers. (We were always lighting up small piles of papers in the same way when we were children. Not budding arsonists, but just having fun.) His typewriter, the Remington Rand, now looking its age with parts of letters rubbed off from constant use (the T missing its crossbar, the S its tailing curve) was set up on a separate table near a high-backed chair. When he wanted to type, and he did so often, he would move to that workstation and then hunt and peck using one finger.

The changes I saw in this set-up saddened me. Mr Pinto had retired and moved to his hometown of Bangalore. The three 'victim's chairs' that used to be arrayed in front of him were gone. Many of his friends had either passed away or had moved to other cities. His cadre of debaters had dwindled. In his retirement, not many mentees came by to seek professional advice. He seemed to be alone in his pursuit of truth. He was not, however, deterred. Nor had he given in to age.

On the porch, he had handed me a legal-sized file folder. It was made of thick cardboard stock, and on its nondescript, light green cover was stamped its pedigree: Sunbeam Office File.

'This is for you,' he had said. I looked at the folder and saw that he had written on the top right-hand corner, 'Ajit's Project', in his beautiful calligraphy. The first page, a title page of sorts, has this in his writing: 'My Life History, R.S. Datta, Original Copy, My Thoughts Part 1, ending on 22nd Nov. 1972'.

He gave me the folder in much the same way as he had given me the cabochon ruby ring: without a word. This was typical of my father—he would engage in one-sided philosophical and academic discussions (sometimes against our will), but he would never ask us to do anything. He did not ask me to read it: He simply seemed to indicate that I might find this interesting at some stage.

I remember him once relating an old family adage: 'We Datts never ask for anything, we take what is ours.' In this context, he was implying that he was not asking me to read it, rather he was requiring me to do so (as though it was his natural right to demand this of his son), but without being explicit in his direction, and hoping that my curiosity would make me go further.

'Why did he give you the folder?' Jo wanted to know. 'Why not to one of your siblings? For instance, to the oldest child, your eldest sister?'

'Yes, I've asked myself this many times. I've also asked my sister.'

'What did she tell you?'

'As always, she was direct.'

My sister had told me, 'You were the only one among us who could discuss things with him. We never spoke up when he asked us what we thought of a point of view he had concerning philosophical matters. You always had an opinion, and, at times, you took an opposing view.'

'Remember,' she said, 'the two of you discussed the nature of good and evil and why evil always seemed to dominate? You took evil's side, and he was for good. That whole dinner the two of you were going back and forth, and, it seemed to me, he was enjoying your pushback. Maybe, because of that quality, he entrusted you with the folder. He always considered you the clever one and encouraged you to view matters from all sides.'

In my childish way, I also tried to match wits with him. On one occasion, I remember, my brother-in-law-to-be was having dinner with us. I had just finished reading a Western novel in which the word 'chute' appeared many times. I tinkered with the pronunciation in my head. Said aloud with a 'sh' sound it was a sloping channel. However, if pronounced with 'ch' sound, it was the Punjabi word for vagina. I asked my father over dinner, in front of all my family, which way to pronounce it, demonstrating both ways. He looked at me for a long time in the sudden hushed silence. 'Let's talk about it later, shall we?' he said.

I knew I had made a mistake, and I pissed in my pants. He never raised it again, though. I don't know whether he forgot, or whether he knew my mortified reaction was enough.

'What was in the folder?' Jo asked me.

'Right at the beginning is a section, about twenty pages long, of legal onion skin paper that crinkles as you turn it, filled with single space type. In it, he described not only his family background and his earlier years but also some details of journeys that he had undertaken with the family as it relocated from one place to the other. It shaped him as an adult.'

Jo wanted me to elaborate on my father's mental make-up, what defined him as a man.

'His family and the family's lineage defined him. His nurture in Baluchistan defined him. If I could boil it down to three things, they would be, first that he was a Mohyal, second that he was a Sikh, and third, that he lived by a code that is captured in one word of Urdu, *ghairat.*'

'You'd better explain.'

'We, and I mean the Datts, are descended from Dronacharya, who was a Brahmin warrior and teacher; he fought in the epic battle of Mahabharata for control over northern India in approximately 1100 BCE. Traditionally, Brahmins are the highest caste of the Hindus.'

'Like the East Coast elite. Around here and in Boston, we call them Boston Brahmins, inferring old money and wealth.'

'In India, the Brahmins are known for being educated and well-read, and their caste was traditionally the intelligentsia of the country, guiding the kings. Our sub-clan of Datts are part of a larger clan called the Mohyals, or "rulers of the land".'

'But you just said, the Brahmins don't rule.'

'True, but the Mohyals were exceptions: they were soldiers as well as being educated.'

'How do you go back to 1100 BCE? I'm hard pressed to go back more than a couple of generations.'

'Our lineage, from Dronacharya, is supported by oral histories and written texts from as far afield as the Levant, modern day Iraq, Saudi Arabia, Afghanistan, and the North-West Frontier provinces of pre-partition India. One of my father's books, which I now have, is *The History of the Muhiyals: the Militant Brahman Race of India* by

T.P. Russell Stracey. Published in 1911, it cites many source documents about the Mohyals.'

I had brought the book with me and showed it to Jo, pointing out a section.

'Look at this. To me this describes a large part of my father.'

> The Muhiyals moreover have nothing, or very little, in common with the orthodox Brahmans. The former as a class do not accept charity (dan) and their pursuits from time immemorial have been either agriculture or the army. They specially reprobate three things (Rawalpindi District Gazetteer of 1907, page 78, Appendix III), viz., the acceptance of charity, the handling of scales (bania's work) and living a life of idleness.

'Another part of the Mohyal lore deals with Alexander the Great who fought and defeated King Porus on the banks of the Jhelum River in the Punjab in 326 BCE. Porus was a Datt. Alexander was so impressed with the valour and hauteur of Porus that not only did he return his kingdom to him, but he also gave him additional lands. Alexander then turned his back on India and left for Alexandria and his death.'

'But why was being a Mohyal important to your father?'

'Lineage, for one. The Mohyals were warriors, people who went against the grain, individualistic people who were Brahmin by caste, well read and intellectuals, but who were also soldiers and kings born to rule.

'The second pillar for him was being a Sikh. He and

his siblings took being a Sikh personally. The founder of the religion, Guru Nanak, had settled near where my father's ancestors lived. In Kartarpur, on the Bain River a tributary of the Ravi River, Guru Nanak set up a new town for the growing Sikh community. He went to nearby villages to preach, and he also went to my ancestral village of Viram Dattan. There he asked my great-great-great, I don't know how many greats to put here, but around the early 1500s, he went to our village and asked my ancestor to make his eldest son a Sikh. My ancestor complied and from that moment onwards, our family has been Sikh. My father and his siblings take this personal request from Guru Nanak seriously.'

'I'm beginning to understand the Sikh strand, but I'm still confused about the Mohyal connection.'

'Remember, earlier on, I told you about the Sikh's tenth Guru, who required all of us to have long hair?'

'Yes, I do, to make you stand out and stand up for your religion.'

'Exactly. A large part of his vision was to have Sikhs be identified as soldier-saints. They were required to be saintly, in following the Guru's teachings, and in consciously attempting to seek God. Thus the long hair, which in India denotes saintliness and a relinquishing of worldly things. But they were also required to defend their freedom to practice a new religion. Defence requires a willingness to fight, to be a soldier.'

'Like being a Brahmin and a warrior. Like a Mohyal. I think I get it now. And what was that third thing you mentioned?'

'*Ghairat.* My father explained it to me one evening. While it intrigued me, it smacked of tribalism.'

'Yes, it sounds very medieval.'

'It does to me, too. But that's the atmosphere in which he grew up, in Quetta and Baluchistan, and he absorbed it. He remained clannish. Taking care of his family was a matter of personal responsibility and identity.'

'I'm beginning to understand him a bit more. I can see the three pillars of his makeup. I don't know if my mother saw them. Or perhaps she did, but did not think that it would be stronger than her love for him, or his for her.'

'Besides these three pillars, one thing above all I remember about him was that he was a very physical man.'

'Yes, I remember him being imposing. My mother described a fight he had with some people by the Buckingham fountain in Chicago. She also said he had told her that he trained as a wrestler.'

'Yes. He writes about that in the folder. All this happened in Hoti Mardan. In fact, my father's physical strength never left him.'

'How so?'

'Even at the age of seventy-five, a few months before his sudden death, he exuded physicality and strength. When I was visiting my parents in Jamshedpur, in January 1974, we were sitting, one day, on the back patio under the pleasant heat of the winter sun. My father at that time walked with a cane because of those cataracts. There were, on that day, three very large, muscled labourers working on the patio under my father's direction. They were trying to dig out the wood frame of a wide, steel-barred set of three windows. It was approximately nine feet wide by about four feet high, and the window was set about three feet above the floor of the patio.

'The frame had been eaten by termites and needed replacement. In constructing the house, my father had used a lot of cement, and the frame was deeply embedded in the wall. The labourers had chipped off the cement, but the frame still held firm in its bed. The three labourers together could not get enough leverage, nor had they the strength, to pull out this frame. After a frustrating time, my father stood up against the admonitions of my mother. He directed his best labourer, a huge man with rippling muscles called Lobo, to place him at the centre of the frame. Once situated like this, he gave Lobo his cane and told the three labourers to step back. He took hold of the bars in the window and, gripping them tightly, he jerked at the frame and tugged it loose. Then he turned around, with the frame in his hands and said to Lobo, "Now the three of you can hold it and put it down in that corner." Then he went back to his seat and resumed drinking his tea. There wasn't any indication that he had just done what three men, a quarter of his age, could not do.'

During that same visit, my mother and I were sitting on the front veranda as the sun was going down. My father had gone for a walk on the golf course in front of our house. She told me he regularly went out towards sunset and walked for an hour or so. My mother would sit there and watch out for him, afraid that blind as he was, he would stumble and fall.

Running through the centre of the golf course, diagonally, was a well-trodden footpath, used by labourers as they walked back from the town and the steel company to their houses by Rivers Meet.

Once, she told me, she had seen my father on the golf course several hundred yards away, in an altercation with two younger men on that path. She was agitated and was about to go to him when she saw that he had resumed his walk and was returning. When he got back, she asked him what had happened. 'Why were you fighting with those two young men?'

'Oh, it was nothing,' he said.

'But what happened,' she insisted.

'Well, I was walking peacefully on the path. These two men were behind me, and they made some nasty joke about a blind, old man with a cane obstructing their way. So, what could I do: I turned around and beat them up! Then they ran away.' He said this as naturally as if he were recounting a sunset.

'But, you're half blind, either of them could have pushed you, and you would have fallen and hurt yourself,' my mother said in an alarmed voice.

'Oh, I never thought of that,' he said, 'how about some tea?'

'Almost exactly what my mother related to me! That was what she said to him after his fight at the fountain. And exactly his reaction. Some things didn't change, did they?'

I told Jo that I remembered how his physicality, and his attitude of mind over matter, impinged on our lives as youngsters.

My father always enjoyed walking. I remember that at the early ages of ten and eight, my brother and I dreaded Sundays when my father would sometimes suggest that we go to a friend's house with him. Instead of driving, he would suggest that we walk there! That the friend lived about five miles away was of no consequence. So off we would go, reaching our destination some two hours later.

There were no sidewalks anywhere, so we walked on the macadamized road which had dangerous cambers. Cars, trucks, bicycles, motorbikes, Vespa scooters, cycle rickshaws, hand-pulled carts, cows, all shared the road with us, so we would have to be carefully looking back and around us as we walked.

Our route used to take us down the slope of our road to the end, where the Garam Nala, the dirty canal, flowed, a stream formed by the water that was used to cool off the blast furnaces in the steel mill. There we would turn left and make a quick right up Straight Mile Road, to the market in Sakchi. At the huge Sakchi traffic roundabout, we would turn right and go past the Basant Talkies where Hindi movies reigned supreme, and past the Punjabi Refugee Colony, where Sikh refugees post-Partition had set up a multitude of very successful food, clothing, and other shops.

The route would also take us past the food cart of a Sikh chef who served aloo tikkis smothered in a tangy chickpea curry with slivered onions on it. I loved this food. He also made dahi bhalla drizzled with a sweet tamarind-based chutney and a coriander-mint hot chutney. We did not stop for that because my father eschewed such street food.

We would walk past the Sakchi Sikh gurdwara, which my father helped establish, though he never went there anymore, and we would then approach the hills made of slag, the waste trundled out in open rail cars from the ever-present steel plant and unceremoniously dumped over the side. There was always a metallic, sulphurous smell that hung in that area. At the hills, we would turn left on Golmuri Road and pass the Golmuri Club and the Golf Course (both lesser rivals to the Beldih Club near our house) and reach the Indian Steel and Wire Products Co., owned and run by a well-to-do Sikh family.

My father would give us advice as we walked. Once he said, 'I'm training you physically and mentally.'

'Why?' I inquired.

'Because I want you to grow up being self-confident, and if one day I tell you to go and conquer Tibet, you won't hesitate. You'll do it.'

Tall order, I thought. And why Tibet? What had they done to us? But I just nodded and strode on.

Our destination, the Wire Products colony, was where three of my father's close friends lived, all on the same street. They were all Sikhs. They would convene, and my father would get straight into whatever aspect of Sikh philosophy he was tussling with.

We would be given a cold nimbu paani or a cooling salt-and-pepper lassi, and we'd run out to find the children on the street and play pickup cricket or soccer or hockey—whatever the sport of the season happened to be. Lunch would be served at about two and, after a satiating meal we would be driven back to our house by one of his friends.

My sister, too, remembers going on similar long walks with him. She told me, 'When we would come back, he would bring warm water in a small basin, mix in Dettol and soap, and wash and massage my feet. Then he would put fresh socks on my feet and tell me to go lie down and rest for a while.'

Both my brother and I had some physical weaknesses and disabilities as children that my father, a strong proponent of mind over body, set about to correct. My brother had quite a lisp. My father's cure was to have him pack his mouth with some marbles and run while 'gargling'. Within a few months, my brother stopped lisping. Whatever had stymied him in his speech was cured. 'Demosthenes,' my father used to say, 'learned to orate this way. He used to put pebbles in his mouth and recite verses while running or walking uphill.'

I, on the other hand, was chubby and prone to bronchial attacks. Every winter, when the temperature changed, dust would swirl around (after having been damped down by the monsoons), and wood fire smoke would haze the evening sky, I would start wheezing. My father's 'cure' was appropriate. He hired a coach to come every afternoon to play field hockey with me in the nearby Keenan Stadium (this was always open to the public and was less than two minutes away).

I remember chasing down hard-hit balls. I also remember that I loved it as it challenged my competitive spirit. Most of all, though, I remember the sweet smell of the red, gravelly earth, or *moram* as we called it, on which we played, and which would discolour my socks and shoes much to the chagrin of my mother. Or, if I fell, it would leave long red streaks on my shins and, perhaps, shave off some skin as well.

My father also enlisted the help of one of his young mentees, who happened to be a champion sprinter, to come to our house to work with my brother and me. Gurbax Singh would arrive, in a roar, on his thunderous motorbike and walk with us to the stadium. There, we would do sprints, laps, and other nasty exercises. My bronchial attacks ceased, and I lost a lot of body weight.

Some Saturdays, my brother and I would be awakened early by our father, and the three of us would go to the Stadium. There, while we ran laps, he would walk the perimeter of the stadium. After half an hour or so of this, we would go back home and do push-ups, squats, jumping jacks, waist-bends and other body-weight exercises. Just like father used to do to prepare himself as a wrestler. The only thing that kept me going was the thought of a delicious breakfast prepared by my mother.

My father practised what he preached: his prescriptions for self-healing included trials on himself. Once he stubbed his big toe, and it turned black and blue with a sprain. Our gardener was tasked with going to the local cavalry barracks to get fresh horse manure. My father would tie up steaming heaps of this in cloth and wrap it around his foot and toe. 'It provides deep heat to the injured part,' he would explain. After a day or so of this malodourous treatment, we begged him to stop, and he did.

On the few occasions he fell ill, he would call our family physician, Dr Biswas, who had a practice on Bistupur Road. Dr Biswas was a rotund man, with a large cherubic face cascading down double and triple chins to his chest, and he was given to wearing safari suits before they were the rage. He also wore square, thick, black-framed spectacles. He would arrive in his Austin and proceed to have tea with my father who would tell him his symptoms as well as what medicines he needed from the pharmacy. Dr Biswas would hum and haw and perhaps alter them a bit but, by and large, he would agree with my father and have them sent over.

Once my father had a deep chest cold and decided to eat raw garlic to cure it. That, too, lasted a day before he was stopped by us. His favourite remedy was for a common cold. He would have a pulao made with equal parts of rice and ghee and eat it all up. As he explained it, to our bemused looks, the ghee created heat inside the body that thwarted the cold. We took all this with a pinch of salt.

One time, I was subjected to his self-treatment ethos after I had come off a bout of jaundice. Dr Biswas told my father that I needed some medicine to improve my liver function. My father brushed him aside as he had his own idea of what I needed. The cook was ordered to fry up a small portion of liver every day and serve it to me with lunch. I could not eat the rest of my meal until this was finished. It tasted awful. But I developed a technique of chewing on the liver and then thrusting it deep into the side of my mouth like a squirrel. Then I would eat my lunch. Away from his oversight, I would spit out the liver. Disgusting. To this day, I can't stand offal.

'My mother told me your father came from a large family and that he was very close to his brothers and sisters,' Jo interjected.

'Yes, my father came from a large, clannish family. He was born in Ghansia, in his mother's parents' house, on 13 March 1899. It was the custom at that time that the expectant mother returned to her parents' to deliver her child. My father was one of nine siblings born to Gopal Singh and Bhaiyan Devi Datta, nee Bali. The Balis were also Mohyals and, therefore, from the same *baradari* as the Datts.'

'*Baradari*?'

'*Baradari*, or brotherhood, is a distinct and important notion that enlarges the circle of one's immediate family through a larger concentric circle of relatives, then further afield to a sub-clan, and on and outward to the larger orbiting circle of the clan. All within that *baradari* are one large family. A tribe.

'Bhaiyan Devi came from a rich family, and this may also have been a reason for the arranged marriage between the two powerful clans, the Datts and the Balis.'

'Why would that make her suitable?'

'The Datts were a prominent clan, but my sense is that they were not very rich. She would bring riches; they would bring reputation to the marriage.'

Bhaiyan Devi is described by my father, in that folder,

as a '*blonde with blue eyes*'. Gopal Singh, he described as '*of average height, being five feet nine inches, dark, broad-shouldered and very strong*'. He also had smallpox marks on his face and a prominent nose, which my father called 'the Datta nose', because it is a common feature of the Datta clan along with a very broad forehead. My father also remembered his father's '*strong hands and arms as he washed my long, unruly hair*'.

'Gopal Singh took his family to two or three places before he settled in Quetta, the capital of Baluchistan, and the city where the British had decided to make their administrative and military base.'

'Does your father say anything about these travels in his folder?'

'Yes, in fact, the first part of the folder is all about these travels. For instance, the first one is when Gopal Singh left the Army. My father writes that he took his family '*by camel to the heart of Baluchistan to the small town of Hindu Bagh*'. Hindu Bagh was halfway from Quetta to Lahore in an east-north-east direction. That journey of 300 miles from the army base where he served at Dera Ismael Khan would have taken several weeks and maybe more.'

For some, the thought of a camel journey across a rocky desert, on the cusp of a new century, may evoke romantic images. The reality, I am sure, was quite different: the uncomfortable, monotonous ride; a newly-born child, my father, tied up in bundles on my grandmother's lap; the vast unchanging landscape shimmering in the high heat of summer; a hot wind; the uncomfortable nights.

My father relates the story of his older brother, then

about three, getting lost the day after they reached Hindu Bagh, when he went outside to urinate. When he had been missing for several hours, Gopal Singh '*accompanied by two horsemen fanned out to search for him. An old woman said she had seen the boy an hour earlier. He was found, fast asleep under the full sun, in the rocky desert-like habitat of that area, unable to speak because of his parched throat. The old woman was asked for water but refused to give it for free. She demanded a rupee (a large amount at that time) for a half glass of water, water being very scarce in Baluchistan*'.

Sometime later, the family moved to Pishin, a predominantly '*Muslim town*' with '*mud-built houses and broad streets*'. Pishin was halfway between Hindu Bagh and Quetta. As my father writes, one of the games the local Pathans played in Pishin was a version of '*marbles that used a hitting stick: except that the marbles were made of sheep vertebrae, and the hitting stick was made of a cow's vertebrae.*'

'Were there any more moves?'

'Yes, to Hoti Mardan before the family finally settled in Quetta. On that move in 1906, to Hoti Mardan, the family went by train—it took four days and four nights to reach Lahore and then another two days and two nights to reach Hoti Mardan.'

'Did these moves have an effect on your father? Did he feel unsettled?'

'I'm not sure how he felt. We never talked about it. However, I'm sure he felt fully taken care of and trusted his parents to do right by their family. I think that the moves from one city to another brought the family closer. They would have only each other for support on those moves. When they finally settled in Quetta, Gopal Singh built a two-storey, brick house for his family. For a long time, that was the only two-storey brick house in Quetta.'

'He must have been well off to have afforded that house.'

'I think he was, but he was also a spendthrift. That's where my father's trait of spending freely comes from, I think.'

'Did you ever go to the Quetta house?'

'I was taken there when I was a toddler so I don't remember a thing. But the Quetta house was deeply personal to my father and an important psychological foundation for him. He grew up in that house, and so profound was its impact on him that, years later, he built us a house in Jamshedpur with similar features. In his retirement, he recreated his childhood.'

TWENTY-TWO

Southport, Connecticut, 6 August 1999

'Did you ever travel by train in India with your father?'

'He took me on a long journey, once. In the summer of 1956, I think it was.'

'Just you? And why was that?'

'At that time, I didn't think about it. However, my thinking now, prompted by my eldest sister's comments, is that I was the oldest male in the house—the heir apparent. He took me on that trip, I think, to show me the world and its ways and to introduce me to family members I had not met.'

'Where did you go?' Jo kept probing.

'I remember taking a train with him to Banaras...'

'The burning Ghats of Banaras?'

'Yes. I was probably twelve when we took that journey. I have only a few memories, but I do recall my father standing up for my obstinate ways a couple of times. The first was on our train which had a fancy name—something like the Amritsar Express, or the Howrah Mail, or, maybe, the Toofan Express (toofan being the Hindustani word for a high wind, though the train never travelled fast at all). We were in a compartment meant for four passengers. The compartment had four bed-sized seats, two lower berths and two upper, which could be lowered when needed and which hung from steel chains. My father and I had gone into an empty compartment. He took one lower berth, and I sprawled over another. At a stop, two more passengers came into the compartment. One of them asked me to move to an upper berth. I refused. The man turned to my father and complained about my lack of respect for an elder. My father said, my son was here first and if he wants that berth, it's his. You take the upper berth. The man saw that my father was not one to be argued with and complied.'

'You stood your ground and your father backed you. That's great. That must have made you feel good.'

'It did. He was not treating me as a child but as an adult who chose not to defer to a real adult.

I also recall that there was no dining car on those trains at that time. People would take their food with them in stacked tiffin boxes. My father and I did not have food with us, but such was the glory of travel that we didn't really need any. At a major station, uniformed waiters got on the train and took our orders for a meal, either vegetarian or non-vegetarian. At the next major stop, an hour later, another uniformed waiter got on with stainless steel trays that resembled TV dinner trays, with little compartments for food. I had ordered a non-vegetarian dinner which had a pile of rice, a couple of chapattis, a vegetable dish, a lentil dish, and a meat dish. There was also a yogurt raita and a dessert. Maybe some pickles. I ate this dinner, balancing the tray on my lap, or on the seat next to me, as the train jostled along in a rhythmic clatter. By the time we had finished, we'd arrived at another station, and a new set of waiters got on and took away the empty trays. Meanwhile, tea servers were plying their wares in loud bass voices, trolling along the platforms. Tea would be served in unfired terracotta cups. The tea, I remember, was always steaming hot, strong, laced with sugar and milk. Delightful. The tea served these days on platforms in flimsy plastic cups tastes different and quite awful. I savoured the terracotta tea as I leaned against the window watching the dark countryside whip past. Occasionally, villages flew by where wood fires burned and huts were lit by kerosene lamps. Now and then, the train engineer would sound the train whistle, and I would hear it disappear, screeching into the wilderness. The click-clack of the train's wheels slowly forced my eyes closed, and I was rocked through the night by the movement of the carriage.'

'What else do you remember?'

'The priest in a major temple in Banaras. I don't remember which one it was, but he kept directing me from one idol to another insisting that I put down a donation at each. I refused. He got very angry with me and went off to my father to complain about my idiocy and lack of respect for the gods. My father simply smiled at me, turned to the priest and said, "He knows what he's doing. Neither you nor I will force him to do anything he doesn't want to do." The priest stalked off in a huff, no doubt, consigning my soul to everlasting reincarnation. I remember my father patting me on the back, as if to say, well done. I puffed up.'

'Once again, your father supported you in the face of an older person. What did you learn from that?'

'Stand your ground and don't give way to authority if you think you're in the right.'

'Wonderful. Anything else?'

'I do remember walking across the Ganges.'

Jo was incredulous. 'You walked across the Ganges?'

'Yes, in the summer, it had dried to a trickle in places, and we were able to wade across it. The rest of the riverbed was sandy. I also remember a cloying smell in the air and asked my father what it was. He told me it was opium, and they were using the poppy flowers to make it.'

'Were drugs widespread there?'

At that age, in those innocent days, I didn't even know what opium was, let alone the use of drugs. The only drug I had heard of was bhang, a milk-based, marijuana-infused drink, made around the time of Holi. I had not heard of other drugs.

'Where were you going?'

'To a small town called Ghazipur, not far from Banaras. My oldest uncle's wife hailed from there, and my father took me to see a part of the family I didn't know existed. My uncle's wife had died in the Quetta earthquake, in the mid-1930s, and I think my father and his older brother were the only ones from our family who kept in touch with her family. We spent a night there. I remember an excellent dinner and that one of the daughters of that household, who was in her late teens, entertained us by playing the sitar.'

'Did you go back to Jamshedpur, then?'

'Oh, no, it was quite an extended trip. Next, we went to Delhi and spent a few days with my three uncles who lived there. From there, we went to see my oldest uncle in Jullundur where he had retired. His driver drove the three of us around in my uncle's big car. We drove, I think, to Amritsar to visit a deceased uncle's family. I remember that that family was the most loving I had ever met, and my aunt, a gentle, elegant woman, who was a headmistress of a school, cooked the most delightful meals. At the end of each meal, knowing I had a sweet tooth, she would make a fresh phulka, slather ghee on it and heap some unrefined sugar from cane juice, *shukkar* as we call it, on top. She would crumple up the phulka with its contents and hand it to me. The sweetness of the melted ghee-*shukkar* against the neutral earthiness of the phulka was a delight. We returned to Jamshedpur then.'

'Did your father talk to you about anything in particular?'

'If he did, I don't recall. The trip was his quiet way of showing me the size of the family and my place in it. And the importance of connections. To this day, if I am visiting any city, I will make a list of the family and friends I have there and make it a point to call and talk to them, if not visit.'

'So, he taught you, by example, the importance of family.'

'Yes, because he learned it early himself. My grandfather died, of pneumonia I believe, in 1918. He was forty-five and left behind his wife and nine children. His oldest son was twenty-two; my father was nineteen.'

'That must have been a hardship for your grandmother.'

'I'm sure it was. My father's older brother, became,

as is the custom, the titular head of the family and he, together with his mother, were instrumental in raising his siblings. It's quite remarkable that all of them went to college. The older brother became a barrister; my father, an engineer; followed by a doctor, an educator, a mining engineer, a developer, and a lawyer.

'My father was closest to his older brother. They formed quite a symbiotic team: my father adored his older brother's open and generous personality and his humble nature. In fact, he wrote a book around him, centred on how his personality perfectly matched the Sikh ideal. My uncle, in turn, was in awe of my father's intellectual mind and his fearless nature.'

'And you? Did you like your uncles and aunts?'

'I did. I particularly liked my *Tayaji*, my father's older brother, but then he was universally liked by everyone. My uncle had a ritual: he would have two measured pegs of scotch every evening before dinner.

'In fact, there was almost a ceremonial nature to this ritual. We never questioned why he drank alcohol while nobody else in the family did. About this ritual, which also took place when my uncle visited us, my father writes in the folder for me, "*Ajit would order pakoras*" from our cook. My mother would also have asked the cook to make the pakoras of batter-dipped, deep fried vegetables. Sometimes we would get samosas, papads grilled on an open fire and served slightly charred, or shammi kebabs served with a coriander chutney. We would have raced through our homework, and then we would all sit around my uncle and watch him as he savoured his scotch, and my father drank his tea, and my uncle urged us to eat the snacks with him. He would tell us stories of our extended family and even inquire about ourselves. In that way, he was more curious and interested in our affairs than my father was.

'His older brother's ritual drinking, my father explained to me once, was because he was troubled by the loss of his beloved wife and daughter in the Quetta earthquake. He too was buried under the rubble and the rescuers reached him at almost his last moment. Those two measured pegs of scotch helped him settle his fears.'

I am not sure how much of that is true, but I do know this: on the occasions that my uncle would visit us, he and my father would sleep out on the veranda. As a special privilege, I too had a small bed made up on the veranda where I would sleep, next to my uncle and my father.

The two brothers would talk late into the night. I would lay awake hoping that they would sleep soon, but I was also curiously comforted by the drone of their voices. Being retired and widowed, my uncle would visit each of his siblings annually and carry detailed news of them and their families to the other siblings. My uncle listened carefully to any advice my father had. Of course, my father, being who he was, would also interject his musings on philosophical matters and draw my uncle into these discussions as well during those nights.

I listened, half awake, half annoyed, at these talks. Subliminally, I am sure, the importance of family continued to be embedded in me.

Once, I was startled awake by an especially loud snore. It was my uncle. I saw him, in a deep sleep, as his body twisted and turned. His hands fluttered up above his chest pushing some unseen weight. His breath came in short intakes. After three or four of these short breaths, there was a very deep breath and then he fell back asleep.

I was alarmed by this display. What did it mean, I wondered?

When I recounted this to my father the next day, he said, by way of explanation, 'My brother is reliving the earthquake. He, too, was buried under the rubble and the rescuers reached him at almost his last moment. He is re-enacting his efforts to get out from under the dirt. Don't be alarmed.'

In Hoti Mardan, my father had also joined the English medium middle school. On leaving Pishin, he had failed all his exams despite being coached by a teacher '*with long fingers who slapped me hard every time I made a mistake*'. It was '*deemed impossible for a son of Gopal Singh to fail*' so he was given a certificate, anyway, to join the third grade in Hoti Mardan.

I remember, I didn't get off that easily when I was at Loyola High School. My report cards from the school in Jamshedpur, which was run by American missionaries who had been sent there by the Baltimore Mission of the Jesuits, came annually. (The postman would deliver these to my mother, but before handing it over would demand something sweet, it being the custom to do this for someone who brought good news. He had obviously, somehow, managed to peek at the contents of the supposedly sealed envelope.) At Loyola, our report cards reflected our grades in the final end-of-year exams. We were not graded for homework, class participation, midterms, or quizzes. Those final exams consisted of essay answers and encompassed all the material learned for that entire year. You either passed that single annual test and went forward to the next grade, or you failed and were held back. I always passed the exams and usually placed in the middle of the class. There was a place on the report card for comments by the Jesuit priests. The usual comment I got was 'could do better if he applied himself'.

My father, who never went to any of my school functions, who could barely remember which grade I was in, would sign the report card and say, 'you can do better'. There was no haranguing; no questioning as to why I didn't apply myself; there were no strictures placed on me; and certainly, no requirements that I study with him, or with a tutor, to get better grades. Maybe he knew I was getting the best education available in that town. Maybe he knew that I was in a class of exceptionally brilliant students. Or maybe, he was not bothered enough to care.

~

'You've told me a lot about your father but nothing about your relationship with him. Your feelings about him.'

'I admired him, looked up to him in awe in many ways, and, perhaps because of that, I was also anxious about his feelings for me. I knew he embraced me wholeheartedly, but did he love me? I'm not sure. There wasn't any overt display of his love. I guess in those days, fathers never said *I love you* to their sons. As I said, I was also a bit afraid of him, maybe because of his aloof and autocratic ways. Maybe because our mother instilled the fear of God in us about not disturbing him; that made us step gingerly around him.'

Jo registered surprise. 'You're telling me you're not sure if he loved you? And that you were afraid of him?'

'He never knew which grade I was in,' I blurted out. 'He never knew where I placed in the class.'

'But, you just said he signed your reports.'

'Yes, of course he did. I don't think the contents registered, though. Or, at least, that's what I think.'

'Now you sound angry.'

'No, I'm not angry but I wish he had been more, say, attentive. Does that word sound right?'

'You'll have to tell me more for me to see if it is.'

'I was, I think, a regular child. I didn't get into trouble, I had no problems in my studies, I got along well with the neighbourhood kids and my classmates, the teachers liked me, my siblings and I got on well. But from time to time I did act out in tiny ways.'

'For instance?'

I proceeded to tell Jo about how I got kicked out of college.

'I went to college in Chandigarh. This was my first extended period away from home. I was barely sixteen. It just so happened that the head of the college, the principal, was married to my first cousin. They were around my mother's age. He was Oxford-educated, a strict disciplinarian, and one who, perhaps rightly, thought very highly of himself. There was quite often a condescending look on his face. He was always neatly dressed, and when I stayed with them, a few days prior to admission, he came down for dinner dressed in a tie and blazer. I'm not entirely sure, but I think the breast pocket of the blazer had the Oxford coat of arms on it.

'When classes started, I moved into the college hostel along with about one hundred other students. Sometime in the middle of the academic year, a new hostel warden was appointed. He was also the assistant principal of the college.

'The new supervisor felt, I think, that he needed to prove himself to his boss and exert his power over the students. He proclaimed that the curfew, lights out, would be shifted down to 11 p.m. from midnight. Given that our dinners did not end until 10 p.m., we routinely started our evening games of cards, or visiting each other's rooms, to gossip or to plan our little escapades, until at least that time. The new curfew would give us just an hour to indulge. All of us were outraged by this fiat. We decided to act.

'One evening, all one hundred of us hostel residents took off on our bikes to see a 9 p.m. showing of *Mere Mehboob*, a blockbuster movie of that time, at the Kiran Theater. I went along in solidarity. I did not stop to think of the consequences; nor did I consider that the principal was also a relative of mine. I was eager to be one of the crowd.

'The show let out at midnight and, by the time all of us had biked back to the college, it was close to 1 am. We decided that besides defying the curfew, a further protest was necessary. We stood outside the supervisor's house, which was on the campus grounds, chanting slogans against him. I was at the front of the crowd and shouting with great gusto. The principal's house was next door, also on campus. He came out and immediately identified me, along with seven or eight other students. The next day, our small group, all from acclaimed public schools, was summoned to his office and summarily told that after the upcoming University exams, we would not be welcomed back the next year.

'I went back to Jamshedpur, anxiously expecting a confrontation with my parents, especially my father. None came. To this day, I don't know why. Again, was my father forgiving? Did he feel that what I had done was right? Or did he just not care? Perhaps, he wrote it off as a youthful folly, seeing in me a more serious side that he knew would assert itself. In any case, we never talked about it.'

'You'd completed your University exams. Did that mean you were ready to go to the next level?'

'Yes.'

'Maybe he just felt that you'd find another college and start there. It wasn't a big deal was it? Nothing much was lost, right?'

'Maybe not. But he was also a very directive person. He did not interact with me, and yet he directed me.'

I told Jo about a time when my father's discipline came up against my laziness.

I was nine, and Loyola High School had long summer breaks, from about the middle of April to the end of July. During that break, I used to indulge in my favourite pastime—laziness.

In those summer months, we would sleep in the cooler garden because we had no air conditioning inside. All seven of our beds would be laid out, side-by-side next to each other, across the length of the garden. The tall hedges that marked our house boundary provided us with privacy. The peepal tree leaves and the fronds of the two palms, guarding our gate, would rustle in the faint breezes that drifted by. I was usually at the end of the line, nearest the flowerbeds adjoining the driveway. Near me was a night blooming jasmine tree, or Raat-ki-Rani, Queen of the night, as we called it. Its small flowers, in little trumpet shapes, would open at night, emitting the sweetest of fragrances. With each puff of a breeze, the aroma would descend on us like nectar. I would fall into a deep, untroubled sleep intoxicated by the perfume.

Around five in the morning, my neighbourhood friends would cycle past our house and give a sharp whistle from the road, across the hedge. That was my signal to wake up, somewhat reluctantly. The sheet covering me would be wet with dew and covered with very fine soot from the steel mill's furnaces. I would splash water on my face, brush my teeth, grab my swimming gear and my bike (a regular, non-geared, Indian-made Raleigh), and off we'd go, racing one another to the Beldih Club, about a mile and a half away. The club at that time was mainly for the employees of the Tata Iron and Steel Co. and their families.

Beldih Club had a great pool, set within its manicured lawns. By five-thirty, we'd be horsing around in the water, setting up races, diving off the three-level diving boards and generally having fun. Our favourite prank was to swim the entire length underwater, and approach one of the gang from behind and try to yank off his trunks. But, sometimes, we pulled off an unsuspecting person's trunks by mistake. (I made a blunder once by sneaking up on someone I thought was my friend and dunking him. The person who came up, sputtering, was a much older woman, who looked around for the perpetrator. I was long gone and at the other end of the pool by the time her vision cleared. I left hastily that day.)

By eight-thirty or so, I'd be back home, having showered at the club. Breakfast would be waiting. And it was a great breakfast: usually I would have three paranthas, scrambled eggs cooked Indian style (with onions, tomato, and green chilies), and an assortment of pickles—sweet, sour, or hot, or all three. My favourite was a sweet-hot-tangy chutney-like condiment we called *gurmaan* made from shredded green mangos and jaggery, a molasses-type, unrefined sugar made from concentrated cane sugar juice. There was the obligatory glass of hot milk to which I would add copious amounts of Ovaltine and sugar to mask the flavour of the milk. On some days, instead of eggs, there would be leftover black daal, a creamy, buttery delight. There is nothing closer to perfection than a hot, crispy, fresh parantha with cold black daal from the fridge.

After this heavy breakfast, I would settle in a chair in our drawing room and read. Our school had a very large library and my list of authors, at that age, ran from Sir Walter Scott to Agatha Christie to Arthur Conan Doyle to Wodehouse to Dickens and, sometimes, to Shakespeare. I read everything with great gusto. We were required to turn in two or three book reports each year at the end of the summer break, but I was usually done within the first fortnight. The rest of the time, I read for pleasure.

At around twelve-thirty or so, my reading would be interrupted by lunch. This was also a heavy affair. There would at least two vegetables, a daal, and perhaps meat. I would eat this with four or five chapattis, accompanied, as usual, by at least three different types of pickles and cucumber raita.

My father, a straight-forward meat and chapatti person, who made his way easily through a stack of chappatis and bowlfuls of meat, disdained my way of eating, chiding me for eating 'like a woman' in a picky manner, that is, insisting on adding all the accoutrements with each scoopful of chapatti. I didn't mind as long as I got what I wanted. And an indulgent mother made sure that I did. When lunch was over, and the others had retired for a siesta, I would make my way to the fridge and select a couple of seasonal fruits which I would cut up into bite-sized pieces. I would spoon generous amounts of fresh, heavy cream from a glass-dish. My mother would skim off the cream that formed as a top layer on the whole milk brought to us daily by the milkman and she would store this in the fridge. I would sprinkle ample sugar over the fruit-and-cream, and relish this happily. It remains the tastiest dessert I know.

After lunch, it was back to the drawing room, a pillow on the floor, the fan going full blast and my book. Fairly soon though, I would be asleep, lulled by the fan, the fullness in my stomach and the sounds of birds and crickets outside.

I would wake at about three-thirty, have tea and snacks, and loll around until five or so when my friends would cycle past my house and whistle to attract my attention.

From 5 p.m. to 8 p.m., it was the Beldih Club again and the same routine in the pool. Sometimes, we would take a break and order snacks and a drink from one of the many, white-coated waiters.

At home, dinner was at 9 p.m. and perhaps the heaviest meal of the day. In addition to the vegetables there would be meat, usually lamb or goat, or chicken, and raita. There would be a dessert of kheer or custard with fruits. By 10 p.m., I would be so sated that I had 'hardly the strength to stagger into bed', as a friend of mine used to say. All was going well that summer when my father intervened.

'I've noticed,' he said, one evening over dinner, 'that you do nothing the whole day except swim, read, sleep and eat.' Our seating at the rectangular dining table was such that my younger brother sat at the head on the only chair with arms. My father sat to his right at the far end of the long side of the rectangle. Two of my oldest sisters sat next to him, then my mother at the foot of the table; next to her, on the other long end, was my seat, and beside me, our third sister.

'What's wrong with that?' I wanted to say, looking around the table. I looked sideways at my mother and caught the silent warning from her. It was just a downward glance of her eyes but that was enough to let me know to not question my father's line of thought.

'I have many books in our library,' he continued.

I nodded. There were books, mostly hardbacks, stored in all possible places at home.

'I'd like to get them leather bound. I have a bookbinder in Sakchi market who does this for me. I'll take you there tomorrow, and he can teach you how to bind books. That way, we'll have matched leather-bound books. And I'll give you one rupee every day for your efforts.' (A rupee at that time was worth 20 cents US.) 'You can go in the morning and come back for lunch. That way you will have accomplished something during the day. You can still swim in the evening. OK?'

Bookbinding was something of a hobby for my father. He had a very heavy, ancient-looking, iron bookbinding press at home that looked, almost, like an instrument of torture. The press had two cast-iron plates about eighteen inches square; the top one was operated by a long screw that must have been at least two inches in diameter. On top of the screw was a four-spoked handle. As you turned the handle clockwise, the upper plate descended, one thread at a time, and any book between it and the lower plate would be slowly squeezed. One of my sisters remembers that she and my other sisters were taught by our father to take apart books, sew them up, put on a cover and bind them using the press. I was clearly not looking forward to encounters with this contraption. I also remember thinking it would be miserably hot and dirty in the bookbinding shop, and that I did not want to learn bookbinding at all.

There was no questioning my father's decision, and off I went the next day to Sakchi and the bookbinder. The bookbinder was as perplexed as I was, and amused, but agreed to train the son of his esteemed patron. I had a rupee note in my pocket.

I saw, immediately, that the shop next door was the most famous mithai-wallah of Jamshedpur, Bhola Maharaj.

I could see the workers busily reducing milk laced with sugar to make the fudge-like barfi that I especially liked. When they had finished, they poured the concentrated khoya into large *parats*, round trays, to set. A few hours later, they would cover it with tissue-paper-thin leaves of hammered silver and cut it into diamond shapes. The rate for a *seer*, about a pound and three-quarters, of these delightful sweets was one rupee! A subversive plan must have developed in my childish brain. I remember thinking that, while I could not say no to my father's suggestion, there was nothing that stopped me from having fun at the same time.

Every morning, I would arrive at 9 a.m. and buy a pound and a half of barfis with my rupee. These I would share with the bookbinder's workers, though I consumed a fair bit myself. I would gamely try to learn how to remove the backs from hardbacks, cut the book into sections, prepare a leather cover, and sew back the whole thing. I was the clumsiest person he had ever known, the bookbinder declared, and I was relegated to the simple task of ensuring that the sections were in order.

We probably got a dozen or so books leather-bound that summer, and I learned nothing of the trade. However, I did develop a lifelong taste for barfi. The output of bound books seemed to satisfy my father, but he also noticed that I was considerably fatter and had developed a strong affinity for this sweet which I kept asking my mother to make at home—an arduous task.

The next year, he let me swim and burn off the excess fat. His well-intentioned plan to help me build some skills may have backfired, but I do remember his firm direction—empty hours needed to be spent wisely and not frittered away.

As I write this, I realize that I never saw my father idle. He was always doing something and doing it quite intently and purposefully. If he wasn't writing to expound on his ideas, he was reading to understand those of others; if he was not doing either, he was passionately advocating his positions on Sikhism or engineering to anyone who would listen; or else he was walking briskly, or methodically sharpening his collection of pocket knives on a whetstone, over which he dripped water every now and then. Even when he spoke to me, he would be standing up and swinging his arms back and forth, exercising. He was an industrious man. Whatever he was doing, he was doing it in a concentrated, determined manner. I think he hoped to impart that industriousness to me, but I resisted, sometimes in passive-aggressive ways.

'He doesn't seem a strict disciplinarian to me,' Jo observed. 'He was just trying to train you to have better habits. What's wrong with that? Didn't you say it was an integral part of the Mohyal personality? Tell me, did you discuss your field of study with him and your career? Did he try to steer you towards a choice?'

'Yes, to both. After I was expelled from Chandigarh, I joined a college in Jamshedpur. My classes ran from about ten in the morning to four in the afternoon. The same six subjects were taught every day. It was excruciatingly boring. One of our professors, a gold medalist student in his own college days, taught us economics. When I say taught, I mean he read from *his* notes from when he was a student learning the same subject. His voice droned over the hum of the ceiling fans. The heat of the day, the whir of the fans, the chattering of students outside in the corridor, all conspired to knock me out.

'I lived for the evenings when I would set off, with three college friends, and stroll up and down Bistupur market, stopping in a couple of cafés for coffee and snacks. The United Coffee House, in the middle of the market, with its cold coffee was always an attraction, as was the Novelty Restaurant, with its array of fast foods, in the Regal Cinema building at one end of Bistupur Road. If the whim took us, we would go to the Madrasi Hotel, almost across the street from the coffee house, and have dosas. We would also pop into stores, managed by fellow college students whose families owned those businesses, for a chat.

'By this time, my father had retired and was consulting with an engineering firm in a nearby city. I saw him during the few days he was home in Jamshedpur.

'He would see me hop on my bicycle and go to college at about nine-thirty in the morning. I would have had a leisurely breakfast and then read the papers. I would return by about 3 p.m. and have tea and snacks or a nap. I did not study. At dusk, usually about six, I would wheel out my bicycle and go over to a friend's house in Bistupur where we all assembled for the evening promenade. His mother would make us strong tea, laced with ginger. After several steaming cups of this, and buoyed by it, we would embark on our haphazard ramble through the market. I would return home by 10 p.m. Once again, he would have noticed my lack of engagement in studies. Once again, perhaps, he felt I had time that needed to be filled with purposeful activity.'

One day he said to me, 'I notice that you don't do anything between 4 p.m. and bedtime. I was talking to Mr Madan and he suggested you join his evening classes at the KMPM School and do a correspondence course in cost and management accounting. It's from the London-based Institute, and it runs from 6 p.m. to 9 p.m. It would suit you in your pursuit of an accounting career.'

Mr Madan was a neighbour and a well-known labour union activist and social reformer, whose son happened to be a fellow member of the promenading Romeo Gang, as we were called.

The accounting career, by the way, was pure happenstance. After returning from Chandigarh and my expulsion from college, my father had sat me down and asked me what I wanted to become. We discussed some options. My mind was not focused on anything.

'Well, I think engineering is out for you since you're not too good in pure mathematics,' he began. 'Your doctor uncle in Delhi tells me you want to be a surgeon, but you can't because he says you're colour-blind.'

'So, what else remains?'

What else remained was precious little. In the social

strata in which I was brought up, there were only so many professions one could aspire to. The dreams of children here in the US, of becoming a fireman, a policeman, etc., were alien to us growing up in India. One had to become a professional earning a decent living.

Another option was to attempt the exams to join one of the civil services: the prestigious Indian Foreign Service, the Indian Administrative Service, among others. But I thought that would be a boring existence.

I said to my father that it would mean sucking up to politicians, knowing that kowtowing was not in his blood.

'Let's forget that,' he agreed. 'No point in lawyering because most lawyers make a pittance.'

In the end my father said, 'You could become an accountant.' He explained the profession to me: 'Accountants keep track of the revenues and the expenses of a business and measure their company's profitability. Because of their extensive knowledge of the company, many of today's corporate heads come from the ranks of accountants and finance managers, especially in America. You have the brains and capacity to do this and become the head of a very large corporation. Like General Motors.'

I was awed by his confidence, though I never had such ambitions. But that was my father: always thinking on a bigger and wider scale. He used to say to me often, in the context of Sikh philosophy, 'The wider your vision, the bigger your truth.'

'All those numbers. It could be a boring job, don't you think?' I ventured hopefully.

He didn't think so.

In the end, of course, I became an accountant.

Again, in the society I lived in, and the prevailing atmosphere, there was no questioning his 'suggestion'.

Now he was suggesting taking on a full load of cost accounting classes in the evening on top of my morning BA classes. Naturally, that's what I did.

So, off I went to college during the day and the correspondence course at night and, over the course of the next four years, got three degrees. In his interactions with me, my father showed a dictum in action: You can better yourself, and you have a responsibility to do it. I remember him saying to me once, 'You're young. You shouldn't feel tired or sleepy. You'll sleep all you want when you're dead.'

Jo then asked, 'What did your father's peers think of him?'

'I don't think he had any peers in Jamshedpur. I think that he himself thought he had no peers. I don't think his contemporaries thought they were his peers. But, if you're asking me what people thought of him, I can tell you. He was universally respected. People were awed by him, especially with his perseverance and single-mindedness, and with his commanding personality. There was no one who matched his encyclopaedic knowledge of subjects. And yet he was adored by people despite their admiration for him.'

'Really? Overshadowing them but still adored?'

'I've run into people, by chance, in England and

here, who knew him in India and who clearly felt he was from a different mould. There was the Sikh man in a gurdwara in London who, on hearing my name when I was introduced to the congregation, came rushing over to ask if I was his son. When I said yes, he almost fell to his knees, and couldn't stop singing my father's praises. A restaurateur in DC started crying when he found out who my father was. He couldn't stop extolling my father. Both also mentioned that he went out of his way to mentor them. That was my father: always wanting to get people to better themselves.'

'That must make you proud.'

'Yes. And then there's the bizarre case of the French teacher.'

'The French teacher?'

When I started college in Chandigarh, I was admitted to the second year of a four-year BA course. The second year, at that time, was when you had to take a University exam. We also had to choose a foreign language. Fatefully, I chose French.

I'd had no French in high school but did have three years of Latin and I thought I could wing it in French. As a precaution, though, I wrote to my father and asked him to send me a small additional sum every month, so I could hire a French tutor. The money came regularly but I took no French lessons. Instead, that money was spent on going to Kiran, the one and only movie theatre in Chandigarh. Near the cinema was the franchise restaurant

Kwality, which served delicious North Indian cuisine and became a favourite hangout. I remember the sense of confidence I had in my own abilities such that, even without the tutoring, I thought I could train myself and pass the French exams. I was worried, though, that if I failed, I would get some punishment, or at least a talking-to, from my father.

The end of the year came and with it exam time. By now, I had already been told by the principal that I was to be expelled. I had not broken that news to my parents, and it weighed on me as I prepared for the exams.

The French exam was split into two portions: a written part and an oral part. The oral exams were presided over by the head of the French Language Department of the university.

About a hundred of us were in a large hall in rows of seats for the orals. At the front of the hall was a large desk with a chair behind it for the examiner. There was another chair for the student examinee. One by one the students were called up. Each one spent roughly three to five minutes in hushed conversation with the professor. After each student left, the invigilator took a few moments to write up his notes on that student. Then he would look up for the next student.

I was nervous because I was not sure how I had fared in the written part of the exam, and I knew that to pass I had to score well on the orals. When my turn came, I went up to the examining desk feigning confidence.

The professor was a bespectacled, square-faced man, dressed in a professor's black gown. His nameplate announced him as Prof Syal, Head of the French

Language School for Panjab University. He had a relaxed smile.

He started questioning me in French: what is your name, describe what you did today, what did you have for lunch, where are you from. All the usual stuff, and I answered these easily. I thought I was doing quite well. Suddenly, the professor asked me if so-and-so (taking my oldest uncle's name) was my uncle. I forgot my French and stammered out a yes. Then, taking my father's name, he said, and is he your father? Even though I thought I was doing well in the exam so far, I was thrown by the new line of questioning. If he knew my family, I thought, and I had done poorly, the news would get to my father and the whole thing of squandering my tuition money on Kiran and Kwality would come out. I was contemplating this with horror but nonetheless managed to speak out that, yes, he was my father.

The professor stood up and walked around the desk. He held out an outstretched hand. He was smiling very broadly.

'I have to shake your hand,' he said.

I got up nervously. By then, he was grinning wildly. I took his hand. He was pumping mine up and down, vigorously. I was dazed. I did not know what the other students were thinking.

He draped an arm over my shoulder and said: 'It is such a pleasure to meet my patron's son. I was your father's cook!'

I was shocked. No, I was stunned and awed at the same time. I knew that my father mentored professionals. But here, before me, was an ex-servant to whom he had given a boost.

Mr Syal recounted the story. He told me he was employed by my father, when my father was part of the team of engineers overseeing the construction of the Sukkur Barrage in the early 1930s. My father was a bachelor, and Mr Syal, now head of the French Language department, was hired as his cook and servant.

A few weeks into this arrangement, my father told his cook that he was unhappy that, from 7 am when he, my father, left for work until about 8 p.m., when he returned, his cook was doing nothing gainful. So he enrolled him in the local school and paid for it. I was impressed at this example of my father using his means, and his will, to direct someone towards betterment.

Mr Syal was grateful for my father's pushing him into education and insisting that he matriculate. Here, in Chandigarh, some twenty-six years later, he was giving thanks to his benefactor's son.

When I told my father this story, he was extremely happy. 'I knew he was capable of much more. Look at the amount of work he must have put in to go through college and become the head of the French Language Department.' (As I told Jo, this kind of story, of vaulting social classes and economic levels, while common in America, is extremely rare in India, almost non-existent.)

I passed the orals, and my enduring hope, to this day, is that it was because of my expertise in French and not because of the esteem Mr Syal had for my father.

I did wonder then, as I do now, why my father never told us that story. Maybe he believed that all good deeds must be done anonymously.

I also wonder what my father would have done had

I failed, and the truth about the misuse of the tuition money had come out. My best guess is he would have turned a blind eye.

~

'Is Sukkur the place where he went when he returned to India from the US?'

'Yes, that was his engineering job.'

'How old was he?'

'He must have been thirty or thirty-one.'

'And even at that young age he had the desire to help people help themselves. I can see why he was adored.'

Looking back at those years, when I was between the ages of ten and seventeen, I was certainly pushing back against my father. There was something subversive in my spending that money on barfis, of eating my way through the additional French tuition monies, as well as my protesting against the college in Chandigarh.

Where, I wonder, did this streak come from? Was I trying to test boundaries? Was I asking for something more basic—such as love or even attention, from an otherwise intellectual and aloof father? To this day, I don't know the answers.

I am reminded of an Urdu couplet by Ghalib:

Kataa kijay na taaluk hum se
Kuchh nahin hai to adavat hi sahi

Don't break your relationship with me
If nothing else, remain my enemy.

~

All my ruminations about my father and my explorations with Jo did not lead in the end to any conclusive, insightful moment for me. I knew him, but I didn't know him. Many of my questions about him, his motivations, his love affair with Louise, his lonely pursuits, were left unanswered. But, when, I realized do we know the totality of anyone?

TWENTY-THREE

Southport, Connecticut, 6 August 1999

As Jo and I resumed talking, I asked if her mother had ever told her about the letters.

'She alluded to them,' Jo said. 'I knew she was a prolific writer, and she must have been sad when he left.'

I mentioned that my uncle had told me a long time ago of a locked trunk my father had in his room in Quetta that was filled with her letters. They kept coming a long time after he returned to Quetta,' I said, 'Almost all the letters from those years are of her undying love and the fervent hope that he would return.'

'Have you read Letter No. 9?' Jo asked me.

'Of course, I have,' I told her. 'You know I've read all the letters many times.' I had filed all the typed copies of Louise's letters in chronological fashion in a binder and had also numbered them.

'Well read it again,' she directed.

Intrigued, I pulled out the binder and looked up #9, dated 9 April 1928. This would have been written three weeks or so after my father had left to go back to India. I read it closely but could not find anything of significance. I told Jo that I didn't know what she was talking about.

'Well, read it again! And this time read it as though you're a woman.'

That perplexed me even more. It also made me feel particularly dim-witted. I re-read it carefully, trying very hard to 'read it like a woman' but at the end I could not see what she was so anxious for me to find out.

She then asked me to take out that letter and read it out aloud. I did, and she directed me to this passage:

'Before I philosophize any more, I must tell you that I am alright now: made a complete recovery! I need not worry any more, now, for a long time—perhaps never, alas!! (Oh but No!! So, I know that unless death takes you—I shall again have "cause to worry" someday!)'

'Now do you get it?'

I had to plead ignorance.

Josephine, talking very slowly and in an exasperated voice said, 'My mother was pregnant! That was the "worry". She either had an abortion or had the child and gave it up for adoption! Can't you see it?'

Finally, I did. 'And in a subsequent letter doesn't she write that the "*problem she had, had been taken care of*"?'

'Now he understands,' Jo said, in a droll manner.

'Did my father know anything about this "worry" before he left? Did it have anything to do with his leaving?' I hoped not.

'I don't know about that. My mother didn't tell me. She also didn't tell me about any half-siblings that I have. She was pregnant, probably with his child. I don't think she went forward with a birth. I don't know of any such child. She probably had an abortion.'

Even as Jo said this, I could sense the doubt in her mind.

'Let me tell you a story my uncle told me, and some of my experiences,' I said. 'Then you can conclude with more certainty.'

Jo nodded for me to go on. I could see she was not convinced but was willing to hear me out.

'My uncle was visiting me in Washington, DC, in the early 1980s. In 1967, he told me, an American man got off a Pan Am flight at Palam Airport, as the New Delhi airport was then called.'

I told Jo what my uncle had relayed to me. Inside, and past midnight, at what was at that time a dingy, chaotic, and outdated terminal, the American man went up to the first Sikh person he saw and asked him if he knew so-and-so, giving my father's name.

The Sikh population in India at that time would have been roughly fifteen million. What were the chances that the person to whom he posed this question would indeed know my father? Pretty slim! The Sikh person he asked did not know my father; but the last name, of Datta, was very unique amongst Sikhs, and he *did* know someone with that last name, who was probably related to my father. He took the American to the person he knew with the distinctive surname, who turned out to be my father's older brother.

My uncle called my father, who happened to be visiting Delhi from Chandigarh. He and my mother were there to help my brother get his work permit for England.

My uncle told him about the American man in Delhi whom he had just met and who wanted to see my father. Intrigued, my parents, along with my middle sister who lived in Delhi, went to the hotel where the American man was staying. I don't know what transpired, and my sister's memory of the meeting is hazy. She remembers a person in his thirties who was a banker.

Most importantly, I told Jo, he claimed he was Louise's son.

'If he was her son, perhaps Louise gave up her child, a son, for adoption? And didn't have an abortion after all,' I said to Jo.

'Oh, piffle,' was all Jo allowed. 'She couldn't have hidden the pregnancy from all of us. Could she?' Now Jo was not so sure about the outcome of the 'problem'.

'What was your father's reaction to this man in Delhi?' Jo wanted to know. 'And your mother's? Was she shocked? Or did she pass it off as something that happened before she knew him?'

'Unfortunately, I was in London at that time and nobody told me about it. Not even my sister. But, in later years, the story was confirmed by two other uncles who lived in Delhi at the time of this encounter.'

'What was his name?' Jo was now curious to find out more.

'All of my uncles and my sister are confused and hazy about his name. They remember him as a Cary or a Gary.'

Jo dismissed this with an 'I don't know any Cary or Gary'. Then I told her of my two personal experiences.

I have been mistaken for another person twice. Each time I was wearing a baseball cap instead of my turban.

Each time, the person I was mistaken for was identified as Larry, or, more fully, Larry Cohen.

I do not know any Larry Cohen.

~

The first time I was mistaken for Larry Cohen was in the early 1980s. My then-girlfriend, now wife and I were returning to Washington, DC, from Toronto where I had taken part in a field hockey tournament. We were in Schroon Lake, a tiny town in the Adirondacks, with an appropriately pretty lake. It was late in the evening, perhaps eleven-thirty or so, and we had just come out of a pub after a distressingly poor dinner.

I was in sweats and wearing a baseball cap. Next to the pub was a pharmacy, with a sign in its window proclaiming that the drugstore was the best 'phamracy' in Schroon Lake. I never did find out if the spelling was deliberately incorrect, more to draw tourists. We were looking at this sign and seeing if there were any other oddities in the display window. There was also a framed sign that read 'Where the hell is Schroon Lake?'

From across the street where there was a group of men, one shouted out at me, 'Hey, Larry! When did you come back?'

My girlfriend laughingly asked me if I had another life and perhaps some aliases.

I just shrugged and said, 'I don't know what he's talking about.'

Then I shouted back to him, 'I'm not Larry.'

He just waved at me and said, 'OK, Larry, if that's the game you want to play.'

At that time, I had the ring but not the letters and certainly no knowledge of the depth of the relationship between Louise and my father. Nor had my uncle told me of the American man at Palam Airport wanting to see my father and claiming to be Louise's son.

In the mid-1990s, my family and I were in Hilton Head, South Carolina. I had just finished a game of tennis and was walking around a small shopping area with my wife and daughters. Once again, I was wearing a baseball cap. We went into one of those ubiquitous shops that sell sodas, tee shirts, sunscreen lotion, etc. There was a long line of shoppers waiting to pay at the only register in the shop. After finding what we needed, I joined the queue.

The cashier craned his neck and looked out past the long line and said to me, 'Hey, Larry! How are you, old friend? You don't have to wait in line. Just come over and I'll take care of you.'

I said, 'I'm not Larry,' but he waved me over saying something like, now Larry, I don't have time to waste with you. Just pay up and I can go back to these customers. Of course, I paid and left.

By this time, I had the ring and the letters, and had read and re-read them. But I still didn't put two and two together. I had not met Jo yet.

'Maybe I look like someone else,' I ventured. 'Maybe there is a Larry Cohen who looks like me when I'm in a baseball cap. My wife thinks I'm spinning a tale.'

'What does your sister say? The one who met him along with your parents in Delhi?' Jo asked.

'When I talked to my sister recently, she confirmed the story, but also told me that she did not have very clear memories of the meeting.'

Jo looked at me for a long time, and then cleared her throat. 'I don't think there's a half-brother that we share. My God, the mere thought of it makes my head spin.'

'Yes, mine too. But, for me, the mystery of the cabochon ruby continues.'

~

I lost contact with Jo. When I checked in with her granddaughters a few years ago, I was told, sadly, that Jo was in the locked memory unit of a hospital in Florida. She passed not long after.

If she were alive, I would have told her of the third time I was mistaken for Larry Cohen.

I was in St Maarten, in the mid 2000s. My wife and I were in a supermarket one day buying groceries for our week's timeshare exchange. I was in the meat section, she in the vegetables aisle. I was wearing a baseball cap, once again.

A man pushing his cart came over to me and said, 'Larry Cohen! What are you doing here?'

I just looked at him. I should have asked him, then, about Larry Cohen so I could have followed up on my own. I didn't.

'I'm not Larry Cohen,' was all I could muster in my surprise.

'Well, come on now, Larry. I know you. You're my neighbour on Cape Cod. Don't you recognize me? What game are you playing?'

I protested that I was not playing a game, that I was not Larry Cohen, nor did I know a Larry Cohen.

'You wait here, Larry. Don't move, OK? I'm going to call my wife.'

With that, he went over to the next aisle and brought his wife to me. 'Who's he, honey?' he asked her pointing at me.

The wife clapped her hands in delight and said, 'Why, Larry Cohen, whatever are you doing here? Why didn't you tell us you were coming down? We could have made plans together!'

Really, I said to both, I'm not Larry Cohen. They inspected me closely and he said, 'OK, maybe you're not. But you're the spitting image of Larry.'

By now, I was in full possession of the facts: I had the ring, I knew its connotation, I had the letters, and I had been educated by Josephine about the possibility of a pregnancy. That was my time, as I think back, to ask about Larry Cohen and get some information so I could link him to Louise. He would have been much older than me, since he would have been born in 1928. Clearly, he had more than a passing resemblance to me. Almost 'a spitting image' as the man from Cape Cod had said.

But I was not aware enough to see the connections, and the chance slipped away.

'You're welcome to your mysteries. Perhaps they keep you on your toes and occupied,' Jo had said that day when I told her about Larry Cohen. 'But the end of their love affair is no mystery. Have you noticed the tenor of the last letter?'

The last letter that I have of this trove, and the one that Josephine was referring to, is dated 25 February 1930. Letter No. 30. This would have been about two years after he left America to go back home. We read it again, together.

It is no longer a letter of passionate love, abundant hope, and resigned waiting. It is a simple letter informing my father of a train accident on 'their old line', the North Shore from Milwaukee to Chicago.

The letter was sent to his Quetta address. Someone, I imagine his brother, had crossed out that address and forwarded it to his new one in Sukkur Barrage.

Beloit
Feb. 26, 1930. 4:30 PM
Rajinder Singh Datta
Hari Kishen Road
Quetta Belouchistan, India
Engineer Setherja (Sind)

Our old route! An auto was hit by our North Shore and bounced into another! Eleven killed and 117 hurt. My mother seems to be making a recovery, tho she is still terribly ill. Peritonitis followed appendicitis which they tell me is as bad a combination as one can find! She is in the hospital, with two nurses on attendance!

Love, Louise

Attached to the letter is a newspaper clipping from the *Chicago Tribune*, dated 25 February 1930, with the headline, 'Investigation of North Shore Electric Wreck in Which Eleven Were Killed Awaits Recovery of Motorman'. The article has photographs with sensational headlines. The train accident had occurred in Kenosha, WI.

The photographs in the article show that all five cars of the train had plunged down an eight-foot embankment, though only the lead car is lying on its side.

'Have you noticed anything about the tone of the letter?' Jo asked.

'Yes, it seems like an incident report. There is no talk of love. Just a wistful reference to their old line.'

'One thing surprises me,' Jo continued. 'While he didn't keep the whole package of 40 letters, he kept quite a few, including the one she asked him to never destroy. He must have been a sentimental person.'

My father had indeed kept this letter. It includes a poem. In its angst-filled brevity, Louise sees herself clearly and her plight for what it is. Reaching down through the generations, it also made one of her grandchildren cry not long ago.

I was in Birmingham, Alabama a few years ago, visiting Louise's granddaughter, Jackie, her son's daughter. I had sent her copies of the letters, and she and I had had some phone conversations prior to my visit. Jackie enthusiastically told me about her relationship with Louise, and that she had been a pupil of hers when she was sixteen.

Jackie wanted to be a teacher. She ended up with a doctorate, and when I met her, had just retired as a professor of clinical psychology at a nearby university.

But at sixteen, she wanted to learn more about teaching. She knew Louise was a teacher and reached out to her, asking what made a good teacher. Louise had sent a long letter about her approach. Jackie shared that letter with me, and said it had really helped her.

In our far-ranging conversation, Jackie told me she was still distressed about a break-up she had forced herself to make many years earlier. Jackie still missed the man, she confessed. She told me that Louise's love affair with my father had moved her. The greatest poignancy and meaning for her, though, was in Letter No. 29. The poem, she said, reflected how she herself felt.

She now turned to that letter, and I asked her to read it out aloud. As we sat around her kitchen table, dusk was settling in outside. The flowers in her backyard were losing their brilliance. The cries of birds were dying out. Darkness seemed to envelop us. Louise's presence and her pathos were palpable.

Jackie read the poem aloud in a quavering voice and eventually broke down in tears.

This is what Louise's letter says:

'*My Darling:*

Many times I have envied this or that writer, the creation of some choice bit. Never more so than now: I have just found this poem by Fannie Heaslip Lea. It seems to me she must have gone through an experience similar to mine—else how could she have written so truly?

It's extremely unlikely that you will want to keep much of all this that I am writing to bear you company on your long journey. But please do not destroy the little poem I offer you today.

Oh darling—darling—darling—I love you so!'

PORTRAIT OF A LADY

By Fannie Heaslip Lea

BECAUSE the world runs on,
She runs on, too—
Steady, she does whatever is to do...
STABBED to the heart, she goes
Straight on her way,
And if she bleeds, the curious can not say—
THEY can not hear the drum
Beat in her brain...
'He's gone—oh, God—he will not—come—again.'

I used to think that my father was not a sentimentalist. That he kept this particular letter, that she asked him not to destroy, belies that belief.

TWENTY-FOUR

Southport, Connecticut, 6 August 1999

'Your father and my mother never met again after he left,' Jo was saying. 'Was it, you think, just a fling for him? I can tell you from my mother's side, it wasn't. She told me as much.'

'I'll get to why I think it didn't work out between them. He wasn't just having fun, in my opinion. Yes, he was alone in America, a single man with no family and, suddenly, here was a desirable woman in love with him and giving him all he wanted. What was there to lose? But, as soon as I thought of this, I discarded it. My father, if nothing else, was a serious person. He was also an honourable person. He would have entered this relationship seriously and after considering the ramifications. I think he genuinely wanted to come back after re-establishing himself in India. So, no, I don't think this was just a dalliance.'

I pointed out my father's concern that he had become too Americanized to be able to resettle in India. 'On board the *S.S. Lahore*, on his homeward journey, he had some misgivings about his ability to re-adjust to India after five years in the US. He mentions this in one of the seven letters he posted to her from Port Said on the Suez Canal.'

'We also know about his reservations through the letter my mother wrote back to him,' Jo countered. 'She had thought of and proposed a solution.'

'There is a sense of desperate hope in that letter, of almost willing a future that could work for them both. But could it have?' I asked Jo.

'Your mother was from a well-to-do, prominent family. She was divorced with two children. She could not live in Beloit with him. Remember also, that she could not marry him, as she could be divested of her citizenship based on the Cable Act. She wanted to live with him, when he was back in America, in a small flat in Chicago, for part of the week, anyway. But it had to be away from her family. She was prepared to be with him in any way that he wanted—even as a mistress, as she puts it in one of her letters. When, and if, she went to India after that, she wrote, she was prepared to live with him in Quetta, if his family would accept her as his wife and a member of his family.'

'Here's what I think he thought. Fact: I am in love with an older divorced woman with two teenaged children. Fact: I have an obligation to her, a commitment of the heart. On the other hand, Fact: I also made a commitment to my mother and to my siblings, that I would earn a degree in the US, get some work experience, and go back to Quetta to help take care of them. This was a shared burden I had with my older brother, of educating my siblings, of taking care of our mother, and of keeping up the family's prestige. This was a commitment of blood and honour.'

'You make this sound like a business decision: do I buy this equipment or that? This was a matter of the heart.' Jo sounded aghast.

'It wasn't just that. It was a matter of principle and obligation. And then there was religion. I think his stay in the US made him more aware of it. He was a Sikh and self-identified with that image. Included were the outward symbols of Sikhism: long hair, a beard, and a turban. His faith in the tenets and philosophy of Sikhism ran deep and had become, even at that young age, a defining quest. Remember in one of her letters Louise writes that, on his return, he could get a job in the foundry but "*your long hair would have to go*".'

'Yes, I remember that. I'm beginning to understand your explanation of his actions.'

'It doesn't end there. He was now an engineer and had valuable work experience. He was being sent back to Quetta, by Bucyrus Erie, as their representative onsite, as a manager on a huge and prestigious construction project. The future was his to make. A job on the foundry floor would have been a backward step and denigrating, don't you think?'

'Yes, if he was at all ambitious, and I imagine he was, then his future in America, what was painted for him by my mother, was no future at all.'

'Except that they would be together...'

'But would that hold? If a man's pride is destroyed, can love sustain him?'

I just looked at her. 'I think we've answered for him, haven't we?'

'Unfortunately, in this case, love did not conquer all,' I told Jo.

'When did he marry your mother?' Jo wanted to know. 'Was it immediately after he got back to India?'

'No. He got back in 1928 and didn't marry my mother until 1937.'

'Where did they meet?'

'They didn't. It was an arranged marriage.'

'Did he know her, or of her? Wasn't he curious about her?'

'He was, and yet he trusted his family to do right by him. An uncle of mine told me that my father was indeed curious and wanted to know what she looked like.'

'He hadn't even seen her? What did he do?'

'His good friend told him that my mother was the principal of a high school.'

'She was well educated for those times. Not an average woman, was she?' Jo had a habit of cutting in.

'No, she wasn't. Anyway, his friend told him, my mother arrived at the school every day in a carriage.'

'You mean a horse-drawn carriage?' Jo was incredulous.

'Yes. Like a fairy-tale princess. Her father was a very rich man, and in a politically powerful position. They had five or six personal carriages at their disposal. My father was advised by his friend to park his car on the opposite side of the road from where my mother alighted in front of her school. He was to pretend his car had broken down. He could get under the car and when my mother got down from the carriage, he would be able to see her.

'He went to all that trouble to see her?'

'Actually, the scheme failed. My father was under his car, and my mother got off the carriage, but on the opposite side from him, and went straight into the school. When his friend asked what he thought of her, my father told him, "All I saw were her ankles. But they are beautiful ankles."'

'Was she beautiful?'

'I'm biased, obviously, but yes, I think so. And she was a feisty woman.'

'Like my mother.'

'Why did he wait so long to marry?'

'I'm guessing here. By 1934 or so, I think he'd decided he was not going back to America and Louise. He may also have felt that Louise's coming to India to marry him was not going to work. He may even have discouraged her.'

'I would say that had to be the case. My mother was so in love with him, and I think she remained that way all her life. Certainly, when she talked about him, I could feel her abiding love.'

'My father probably tried to convince his older brother to let him marry Louise,' I continued. 'By then, of course, the Depression in the US had negated any thought he might have had of going back. He was hoping to remain a Sikh, have a managerial job, marry her and live in Quetta.'

'That would have suited him, of course. But why try to get permission from his older brother?'

'He was the head of the family, and my father would not have wanted to forsake his family. His sense of familial duties was overarching.'

'You told me that you were married before to a European. Did you get your father's permission to marry her?'

I looked pointedly at Jo.

'This is not about me.'

'I'm trying to understand the son: Was he like his father? Did you feel the yoke of your family's customs and demands?'

'Yes, I did. But I rejected them.'

A scene played out before my eyes as I was talking to Jo—a conversation between my older sister and me about these very questions.

I recalled that I had recently called my sister to get her side of the story. She told me, 'Remember when you wrote to our parents that you were coming back to Jamshedpur in 1970 and that you were coming with your French girlfriend? You wrote that you intended to marry her here?'

'Yes, I remember that, and I felt so good that all of you were very accepting of the plan.'

'Wrong,' she said. 'Our parents may have accepted that, but I protested to both.'

'On what basis? Why did you care whom I married?' I was angry.

'We sisters had arranged marriages and I did not like the fact that, when it came to you, a son, you could marry the person you chose.'

'You objected?' I was incredulous.

'Yes, I did. I objected strongly. I made the mistake of airing my opinion at a public gathering and our mother and I had a falling out. She stopped talking to me for quite some time.'

'I didn't know that.'

'No, you never know anything, do you? In any case, that was also the time when Papaji had developed a habit of walking over to my house. We would sit and talk for long periods on my veranda. When you wrote that you were marrying a French girl, I asked him why he did not object. Do you know what he said?'

No, of course, I didn't.

'He said he did not want to lose a son. He wanted to keep the family together.'

Jo understood. 'Your father kept his focus on the family at all times, didn't he?' she said. 'He would have sought his brother's permission to marry my mother, in order not to break with his family; and, in your case, he decided to let you have your way, also in order to not break up the family.'

I nodded.

'If family was important to him, why isn't it important to you? Why not consult with them at least on whom you were going to marry?'

'Family is important to me, very much so. But times had changed somewhat by the time I wanted to get married. My parents had always told me to marry the person I wanted. My marrying someone I wanted was not, in their mind, a rejection of my family.'

'And, yet, your sister's objections were based on fairness, weren't they?'

'You're right. I did tell you, didn't I, that I was the first son after three daughters and that I was treated very differently by my mother? My mother held sway over my father in these matters. He wanted to make sure that I didn't drift out of the family's ambit. And I haven't.'

'In the end, what you're telling me is that your father could have made a go with my mother in Quetta. He could have married her against his brother's wishes but refused to do so. Why had he denied himself in choosing not to marry Louise?'

'He chose family,' I told her numbly.

Jo fell silent and looked at me for a long time.

TWENTY-FIVE

Southport, Connecticut, 6 August 1999

'You still haven't told me how you found me,' Jo said. 'I also don't know how your father succeeded in keeping his thoughts, and especially his younger self, away from you. It was almost as though he had partitioned it off.'

'Yes, that's a good word for it. Compartmentalized, may be even better.'

'Were there any vestiges of my mother in your father's later life?'

'Her piano playing.'

'What do you mean?'

'I remember he asked my oldest sister to learn how to play the piano. None of us knew about his love affair at the time. But around that time, the ring had just arrived and now I wonder if that triggered memories of Louise playing the piano. In any case, my sister, who was in high school at that time, attending the local Sacred Heart Convent School, went twice a week to take lessons from Sister Rosetta, a nun there. She also used to stay after school and practice. She says she became quite good at it and, in fact, passed the first stage exam conducted by Trinity College London. She told me our father would leave work early to come to hear her practice from time to time. He would sit in the back and just listen. It must have pleased him.'

'Do you think it reminded him of my mother playing the piano?'

'Maybe. My sister also remembers that he offered to buy her a used piano for 2,000 rupees. Interestingly, it was my mother who put her foot down and refused to let him purchase the piano. She cited space considerations. But did she know about his affair, prior to their marriage, with the concert pianist? If she did, she probably didn't want the memory of that affair to be a presence in the house in the form of a piano.'

'*Did* your mother know?'

'Who's to say what she knew, what she chose not to know. In any case, it had happened a good ten years prior to her marrying my father.'

'Was there anything else you think he remembered of her later in life?'

'Your mother read the *Saturday Evening Post*, didn't she? My father subscribed to it in India, and I got to read it too. Then there was this wonderfully perfumed hair oil that he used. I think it was called California Poppy Oil. He must have used it in America.'

'Wait! Among my mother's possessions was a half-empty bottle of that oil. I know she never used it. Do you think it belonged to your father and she kept his bottle all those years?'

'Maybe,' I said. I was getting emotional at this thought, and Jo had started crying.

When she was composed, I said, 'Your mother continued to think of ways to be with him after he left, didn't she?'

Josephine had confirmed to me, in one of her letters, that her mother read prodigiously and had a wide-ranging taste in books. She was well informed, and held evening discussion groups with professors from Beloit College.

'When my father went back to India, she relates in her letters how she was reading up all she could about India in newspaper articles and books. In this way, at least, I think she felt close to him and present, somehow, in his life. Do you remember those passages in her letters?'

Jo was nodding yes.

'Your mother read and disliked *Behind That Curtain,* Earl Derr Biggers' racially-tinged Charlie Chan mystery about the disappearance of a woman in Peshawar. The book was serialized in the *Saturday Evening Post* which is where Louise read it. She dismissed it, as she writes in her letter, and scorned Biggers for writing about Peshawar even though she was convinced he never got closer to India than an Indian shop in America.'

'Yes, and someone sent her some material on Katherine Mayo's book, *Mother India,* and my mother condemned the book for its pro-Imperialist and Indophobic bias. She also stopped communicating with that person.'

'In her letters, she mentions attending lectures by a Sikh spiritualist, Bhagat Singh Thind. Do you recall that?'

I asked Jo. 'She attends those lectures even though she knew that my father disdained those he deemed quack preachers.'

'Your father was very strict, wasn't he?'

'It was more that in our religion, proselytizing is considered a no-no.'

'The other way she was with him,' Jo said, 'was by following his journey on a map. I remember in one letter she talks of tracing his journey *in* "National Geographic *for March (which you had marked for me, here in the Studio)*". My mother was certainly smitten with your father. But we'll never know, will we, whether he tried to follow the plans that she had set for them.'

I just shook my head.

Jo had straightened up in her chair, all business again.

'The genealogist gave you nothing more than the census data. What did you do next? I'm still curious how you got to me.'

The genealogist's report had arrived in April 1999. I was despondent at the time, angry at myself for not making any progress in my search for Louise. Feet on top of the desk in my office just outside DC, leaning back in my chair, I thought, dejectedly, what next?

My search was physically confined to the US mail, the telephone and microfilm, as the Internet was not widely available at the time.

At my desk, that day in 1999, I picked up the newspaper and went downstairs to the deli for lunch.

Munching disinterestedly on a roast beef sandwich, I was leafing through the paper when I found the classifieds.

Immediately I thought, how about an ad in the local paper, asking if anyone knew or remembered her. It was a longshot, but I had nothing to lose. I had no other avenues left to explore. This was the adrenaline kick I needed.

I hurried back to my desk and called the Beloit library, asking the librarian which of the papers she would recommend for the ad I had in mind. She told me I should place the 'looking for' ad in the *Chicago Tribune* which had wide circulation in the region. Additionally, the classified ads had just started appearing online on the paper's website.

I drafted a very simple ad, which started 'Seeking Louise Rood Lutes...' Listed, of course, were both my home and office numbers and my email address.

I faxed the ad to the offices of the *Chicago Tribune* where it ran on 22 May 1999.

'In the end, it was just an ad?'

'Yes, just an ad. A lucky break. That's why I told you that luck and serendipity brought us together.'

'Don't forget your steadfastness in the search. Why did you persist?'

'It was a problem. It was a mystery. It was a pursuit. It had all the ingredients of a quest. In the end, it was the excitement of the chase that drove me on.'

'Now that you have solved the mystery of the ring, what are you going to do?'

'I'm not sure. I don't know if there is much more to do.'

'Yes, there is. Yes, absolutely there is. You and I are going to write a book about your father, my mother, the train they met on and the journey of love they embarked upon. We're going to do what our parents didn't. We'll use the forty letters to write their story. That's what we're going to do. Agreed?'

Jo was reaching across the table with her hand extended. I took it and she shook my hand forcefully.

EPILOGUE

Ajit Singh Dutta passed away in 2022.

Although he didn't live to see this book in print, his wife, Bonnie, and their two daughters, Danielle and Nikki, know how much the publication of the memoir meant to him.

ACKNOWLEDGEMENTS

My husband, Ajit, the author of this book, was drawn into the romantic mystery of his father's early life through clues, which revealed themselves slowly, sometimes through great investigative effort on his part, sometimes through pure serendipity. I witnessed up close the writing of this book and can only hope that I was a helpful and supportive partner throughout the journey, along with our daughters, Danielle and Nikki. I know Ajit's challenge was to write a book that, while anchored in true history, needed to be filled in with a good amount of creative imagining. Along the way, he received generous advice, ideas, guidance and inspiration from family, friends, professors, and editors. Since Ajit passed away before this book could be published, I am attempting to honour all of you here, and I apologise in advance if I left anyone out. Please know it was not intentional.

The Dutta family: Ajit's niece, Bandhana (Reema) Bajaj, who safeguarded the trove of letters from Louise to her grandfather and gave them to the author; cousin, Mina Singh, who made the introduction to the literary agent/editor in Delhi; siblings, Kamal Sethi, Kiran

Bakshi, Renu Bhasin, and Ranjit S. Dutta, who shared their memories and were an integral part of the idyllic childhood cherished deeply by the author.

The family of Louise Rood Lutes: daughter, Josephine Lutes Humphreys, whose memories of her eccentric mother, descriptive letters and great enthusiasm for the story were critical to the author; granddaughters, Jackie Lutes Goldstein and Susan Humphreys Klein, for filling in the portrait of 'Granya' Louise; and, granddaughter-in-law, Leslie Lutes, for the miracle of seeing the ad placed by the author in the *Chicago Tribune* in 1999, and then connecting him with the descendants of Louise.

The professors and cohort colleagues at the University of California-Riverside MFA Program, who were valuable advisors, readers and critics as the work progressed: David L. Ulin; Jill A. Essbaum; Gina Frangello; Agam Patel; Tod Goldberg; Art Hanlon; and Pam Munter.

The friends who generously gave their time and shared their honest consideration as readers: G. Hamilton Loeb; Megann Yaqub.

The editors: Evelyn Renold (New York), who worked with Ajit to put the finishing touches to the story and then graciously worked with me to oversee the last round of edits after he died; Saroja Khanna (Delhi), who took the story forward to the publisher and edited the book for publication in India.

The publisher: Renuka Chatterjee of Speaking Tiger Books.

—Bonnie L. Galat
2023